D0370055

The Tao of Horses

Exploring How Horses Guide Us
on Our Spiritual Path

DONATION

by Elizabeth Kaye McCall

▲
Adams Media
Avon, Massachusetts

WEST

DISCARD

22378509

3 2140 00179 8574

SF
301
M2223
2004

Copyright ©2004 by Elizabeth Kaye McCall.
All rights reserved. This book, or parts thereof, may not be reproduced
in any form without permission from the publisher; exceptions
are made for brief excerpts used in published reviews.

Published by
Adams Media, an F+W Publications Company
57 Littlefield Street, Avon, MA 02322. U.S.A.
www.adamsmedia.com

ISBN: 1-59337-099-7

Printed in Canada.

J   I   H   G   F   E   D   C   B   A

Library of Congress Cataloging-in-Publication Data
McCall, Elizabeth Kaye.
The Tao of horses / Elizabeth Kaye McCall.
p.   cm.
ISBN 1-59337-099-7
1. Horses—United States—Anecdotes. 2. Horsemen and horsewomen—
United States—Anecdotes. 3. McCall, Elizabeth Kaye. 4. Taoism. I. Title.
SF301.M2223 2004
636.1'00973—dc22
2004009170

This publication is designed to provide accurate and authoritative information with regard to
the subject matter covered. It is sold with the understanding that the publisher is not engaged
in rendering legal, accounting, or other professional advice. If legal advice or other expert
assistance is required, the services of a competent professional person should be sought.
—From a *Declaration of Principles* jointly adopted by a Committee of the American Bar
Association and a Committee of Publishers and Associations

Many of the designations used by manufacturers and sellers to distinguish their
products are claimed as trademarks. Where those designations appear in this book and
Adams Media was aware of a trademark claim, the designations have been printed in
initial capital letters.

Interior illustrations by Graphic Expressions.

This book is available at quantity discounts for bulk purchases.
For information, call 1-800-872-5627.

To my lifelong inspiration—horses.

Contents

Acknowledgments

THANK YOU TO EVERYONE WHO SO GENEROUSLY AGREED TO BE interviewed for this book. My deepest appreciation for the thoughts and experiences you shared. To Kate Epstein, my editor at Adams Media, this book would not have been possible without your total trust in the creative process. Thank you for allowing me this opportunity to write on the topics closest to my heart. To two other incredible editors who have tremendously impacted my writing career—Alan Capps, my first editor at *Ride!* magazine and Kathy Balog at *USA Weekend*—thank you.

To the kind and wonderful people who are my family, thank you for everything: my mother Patricia McCall, father Frank McCall (who took me horseback riding!), stepmother Libby McCall, sister Linda McCall, nephew Stephen Hall, sister Barbara McCall, and nephew Charles Maxwell Hall.

My heartfelt appreciation goes to Barbara Walleston, who really made a difference. To Jack Smart, Larry Dorn, Ken Khachigian, and Alvin P. Ross, I have not forgotten your help—thank you. To the dedicated staff at Sherman Oaks Library, you saved my day more than once.

Many have helped me on my spiritual path. I thank you all, especially Stephanie Cox, Trade of the Seven Moons, Madeleine Gough, the late Rev. Edward Monroe, Patricia and Jon Diegel, Jon Parmenter, EJW, HYL, and IHHL.

To the horse people in the United States and abroad, thank you for always opening your doors to me. I cherish our friendships. Thank you, Abdule, and to the thousands of other horses who have shared their world with me—may there be many more.

Introduction

EVERY DAY WE MAKE CHOICES THAT CAN CHANGE THE COURSE OF our lives. The afternoon I headed back to BookExpo in Los Angeles during the final hours of the convention was one of those for me. I had pretty much decided to go horseback riding, but then intuition made the case for one more drive downtown, even though the annual gathering of publishing professionals was almost over and I hadn't planned to return again. Two days earlier, I had spent a full eight hours tromping the aisles of the Los Angeles Convention Center and met a magazine editor I had worked with for several years in person for the first time. I thought I'd seen enough. But when intuition called, I listened— fortunately.

Some of the booths were already vacated at the BookExpo when I came upon Adams Media's booth and met Gary Krebs, the publishing director. A single copy of a horse book title still on the shelf soon had us discussing the huge and largely unrecognized United States horse industry, some of the many articles I've written, and my equine-oriented travels.

Two days later, Kate Epstein, a project editor back at Adams Media, phoned from the company's Massachusetts headquarters to see if I might be interested in submitting ideas for a title in development on the spiritual side of people's relationships with horses. I was stunned, thrilled, and convinced the project "had my name on it." Not only did such a topic speak to my personal experience of horses completely, the subject of writing a book had been surfacing for several years from various directions. My nephew Max Hall began asking me to write one when he was eight.

Suddenly, I was in the saddle for a ride like none before. From the moment the contract was signed, nothing went the way I anticipated. Interviews planned specifically for certain chapters veered off in unexpected directions. People I did not expect to be problematic in reaching were unavailable. Some I didn't expect to connect with showed up in Los Angeles unexpectedly. At one point, when I was interviewing Corky Randall, he predicted that there would be a point when I would find a common thread in what everyone I was talking to was saying. His words rang true, but it remained elusive for days.

Finally, when I tossed a few of my plans to the wind and started looking at the hundreds of pages of interview notes as a puzzle, *The Tao of Horses* began to breathe on its own. As I looked at the myriad ways horses touch the lives of people in this book, I could also see how each story represented truths for me.

With that came some well-timed events that a whim or fleeting decision revealed immediate answers to. Near the end of Chapter Four, while I was out running an errand, I stopped in an Italian restaurant in Encino, California, for a late afternoon coffee. The place was empty and I was debating whether the idea of "dressing up" was too strange for the Try This section at the end of the chapter, when in walked a cute guy in a sports jacket, jeans, and cowboy boots. The timing was too perfect. Suddenly, from across the room, I was saying, "Excuse me," to see if he truly was a horse person. (In actuality, he just liked the boots.)

Just as unexpectedly, I met violinist Albert Stern in a computer store in Santa Monica when I stopped in on the spur of the moment. Although I was aware that he owned horses, I had not had the opportunity to meet him. I interviewed him at his ranch the following week for a perfect opening for Chapter Eight.

It has always been clear to me that writing about other people's lives is a huge responsibility. In a book like this it is almost like being entrusted with a part of someone's soul, like a carrier pigeon of sorts, to make sure the spirit of what has been shared is conveyed, or transported, as intended. Because of all *The Tao of Horses* involved, there have been many revelations of the heart, both from those formally interviewed and in the course of conversation with friends.

In the years I have known jewelry designer Maria de la Luz, somehow, we never discussed why she has a horse for the logo of her Pasadena-based company. I knew she was fond of horses, but didn't ride. The subject finally came up while I was writing this book. The logo was inspired by her brother, jockey David Rodriguez, who died at nineteen in an accident on a muddy race track in Colorado. Ironically, he was being honored in that very race for having rescued several horses from a flood two days before. "He had no fear," Maria told me. "His determination and fearlessness have been with me since then. My love of horses is a way for me to keep his memory alive. He has been a great inspiration in my life." Having interviewed two Hall of Fame jockeys for this book, who put their lives and passion on the line with every ride, I was especially touched by her story, as I have been by the many individuals who spoke with me for this project. It has changed my perception of horses in ways I have still not fully realized.

While this book is by no means intended as a training manual, some of the comments made by horse professionals in this book—who do not normally philosophize on the topics we got into—were particularly illuminating to me.

On a personal level, hearing myself talk on the interview tapes brought some revelations too. I was a little embarrassed when I heard my own voice adamantly saying, "Church to me is horses. I'm not kidding about that. That's where I find my peace." However, it's the truth. I believe horses are a doorway to our own humanity and spirituality in a way that is extraordinary and unique.

It's always been this way for me. When I was just eight I wrote a letter to Santa Claus . . .

Dear Santa,

Thank you for the encyclopedias. I use them quite a bit.
I especially like "H" because it has horses.

Sincerely,

Elizabeth Kaye McCall

Chapter One

Presence
. . . the ride of your life

A horse doesn't care about yesterday and he's not worried about tomorrow, but he's darn sure interested in the moment . . .
—James Wyllie

FROM THE CELTIC HORSE GODDESS Epona, to the myth and magic of Pegasus, horses have captivated the human psyche for thousands of years. History has been written astride their backs, civilizations and explorations furthered.

Horse heroes have enlivened film and television—from the Black Stallion to Roy Rogers' Trigger and the wise-cracking Mr. Ed. Others, like the racehorse Seabiscuit, have known a renaissance, as tales of real-life horse legends resurface.

Yet, around the globe in near obscurity, legions of horses transform human lives by virtue of their very existence. Like

1

Taoism, the path of horses revolves around the experience. Presence, a spiritual cornerstone to Buddhists and to best-selling authors, is immediately understood by anyone astride 1,000 pounds of muscle directed by instinct.

Saddling Up

"Horse church" began early for me, somewhere around two or three. I rode my first pony after Sunday school, still wearing a fancy dress and petticoat. The moment unleashed a lifelong passion that steered my college choice, helped land a competitive job in the airline industry, inspired a master's thesis, and has taken me on location from Namibia to Mexico for horse films.

I've heard the clatter of horse hooves on ancient drawbridges, while riding a tireless mount inside the stone walls of French castles. I've been atop a swimming horse in the Caribbean off the coast of Jamaica, sliding perilously to one side as he leaped onto a sandbar. I've galloped the ocean's edge in Acapulco on a spirited palomino, while the late afternoon sun dropped into the horizon, a luminous glow. In Egypt, a noted horse breeder served tea, as her prized Arabians paraded by. Adorned with beaded turquoise necklaces, they wore protection from the evil eye. At Churubusco Studios in Mexico City, I witnessed a movie horse trainer direct an equine actor to move his head with the point of a finger—while hiding from the camera beneath a burlap feed sack. In a wide-open African desert at night, I watched a four-month old filly trained to perform at liberty walk to a foot-square ground marker and stop, after the director yelled "Action!"

Some of the firsthand stories I've discovered when covering horse competitions made the events pale in comparison. I've watched a blind assistant district attorney from New York ride a dressage test to music on a horse she first encountered two days earlier at a national horse show. A mother told me of a doctor's early prediction that her autistic son was destined for life in an institution, as we together watched him in a jumping competition as a teenager. I will never forget the newspaper owner from El Salvador whom I met at a Central American event, recounting how farm workers saved his cherished Peruvian Paso horses while guerrillas ransacked the countryside. He was hours away by plane, hospitalized in Texas after a heart attack. (The horses were herded through a river to safety in Guatemala.)

My own experiences have run the gamut, with occasional fear amidst the joy. I was once aboard a stallion who suddenly reared, lunged, and hurled himself toward another stallion on the opposite side of a fence. At the home of a European circus family, I cued a trained horse to rear to full height just three feet in front of me, by simply raising my arms. Pure joy!

Who could have guessed a pony ride would unleash a path where diverse people, places, and events might intersect?

Trick or treating on horseback as a teenager in Ohio—with hair in curlers—stands out among my Halloween memories. One Christmas in Santa Monica, California, I led an Arabian decked in wings as Pegasus along Main Street, as stunned diners ran from restaurants to see the horse. Cars veered to the curb to take photos—just like a scene from the movies. An idea to literally ride into the new millennium came true at an equestrian center outside Paris on New Year's Eve 2000. Wearing a sequined jacket and black jumpsuit, I rode a chestnut mare at the stroke of midnight, while fireworks exploded in the City of Light.

The Path of Perception

Looking back to my pivotal first pony ride, it seems ironic that my spiritual connection to horses began on the periphery of a traditional church. But writing about my horse-related experiences is serving up memories so filled with synchronicity of this type (and sequels: same story different form) that they might have been scripted in Hollywood. I have also experienced an unsettling revelation. While horses have been a source of inspiration and catalyst in my life from the first encounter, I got sidetracked from following that path by my personal beliefs, not from outside circumstances.

As a young girl, I loved collecting horses, reading about horses, drawing them, even galloping around the playground as one. Whether in pencil, crayon, paint, or clay sculptures, the horse was always the chosen subject of my artistic efforts. This was true, at least until seventh grade, when I butted heads with my first official art teacher.

Before the school year concluded, the art teacher made horse-related projects off-limits for me, banning any further art assignments using horse subjects. Considering the prevailing mid-American perspective on education in the early 1960s, it is conceivable that the teacher intended to encourage me to expand my artistic horizons. However, eliminating horses from my options only narrowed my horizons. The following year I dropped art, thinking, "I'll show her."

Twenty years later, working on a master's degree, I took an elective art course on a whim. Drawing daily for a school quarter revealed enough talent that I recognized I may have cut myself off at the pass instead of finding another way. Did a horse obsession block my artistic talents? Or, did it underscore the importance of inner freedom to pursue the way of the horse in any form?

Writing is a magnifying glass of self-examination, leaving little room for truth to escape.

For the first time in years I recall hiding my riding jeans in a drawer as a kid after returning from the joy of all joys, Wilcox Pony Farm. Safe from the suds of the washing machine, I would pull them out days, maybe it was even weeks, later. Reveling in the faint aroma of horse, I was transported to another world.

The Road to Presence

I've always been intrigued by the mystical aspects of existence, some more sensational than spiritual. At teenage slumber parties we entertained ourselves with Ouija boards and attempts to levitate. When I moved to Los Angeles in 1980 the personal growth/new age movement was well underway. In my travels along this road since, I've studied with a Celtic shaman, a Tiwa medicine man, and a Tibetan Buddhist teacher. I've taken workshops on energy and healing with Howard Lee, Carlos Castaneda's one-time healer. After three years of dabbling on the perimeter, I delved into Ho'oponopono, an ancient Hawaiian problem-solving practice.

During more than twenty years of dream study, horses have appeared as frequent guides. In daily life, horses have most clearly defined the meaning of presence to me—representing a clear conduit for instantly getting the message.

A white Arabian stallion named Abdule, whom I had the privilege to ride for many years, was the master at making the lesson of presence succinct. Like clockwork, the moment I would drift into thought, riding on autopilot, he would make me present again, noticing some item that justified a spin, rear, or leap in his world.

Living for the Moment

"The horse lives for the moment. He doesn't think and prepare for the future. He solves the problem he has to solve at that moment, not two seconds later," remarks James Wyllie, who founded and directed Pepperdine University's Equestrian Education Center in Malibu, California, its entire thirty years of operation.

At last count, the equestrian expert, educator, and philosopher had taught some 60,000 people to ride. "You have to have the same outlook on reality," explains Wyllie, now head of the California-based Equestrian Education Foundation, where reading assignments on Tolstoy, Kipling, and Churchill (all authors of horse stories) combine with riding instruction. "The moment means everything. That's the difference between you and the horse. The horse is a grazing animal, not a predator. To be able to survive, his skill has to be in reacting. He doesn't think to solve problems, he stays alert and gets the heck out of there, 'cause survival's the only thing he's interested in."

Wyllie reflects, "Man and horse are about as opposite as you can get, kind of like yin and yang. Now a predator like you and I, we have to gather information through our five senses, store this in our computer brain, and then we have to be able to recall that when needed and make a decision. That's all terribly time consuming." Wyllie elaborates, "A decision must be made on time. The quality of the decision is secondary. A bad decision can be changed, but being on time cannot. Otherwise, the horse makes the decision and all your control is lost."

Sporting a close-cropped moustache, crew cut, and frequently a cowboy hat, Wyllie's appearance is little changed since he rounded up 180 head of horses a day as co-owner of the Paramount Movie Ranch (now a park) in the 1950s. Wyllie taught President Ronald Reagan's Secret Service personnel to ride, provided horses for the 1984 Olympics Pentathlon, and instructed for ten years at Cal Lutheran University before Pepperdine.

Rethinking Reality

"What we're trying to do is make a brand new animal. The horse is a fugitive that would run away from man, not staying there working with him. He's got to be trained to work with man and man has to be trained to work with them," reflects Wyllie. "Horses make you aware of everything around you and your responsibilities. Nobody would get in a Ferrari and stomp it to the floor before they found out how fast the pickup was. The same is true with horses. You have to learn what you're dealing with."

Wyllie's life with horses was never planned. The Rhode Island–born Air Force veteran flew airborne reconnaissance missions during World War II—first as an observer and later as a pilot—although he took a brief course for people who couldn't ride while in the service. "You had a choice, learn to ride or walk eight hours a day," he recalls.

Wyllie was well into a postmilitary industrial design career when he landed a project to build a horse stable that wouldn't burn. Fall brush fires are common in the hillsides around Los Angeles. He began running the completed facility on a temporary basis when the manager never showed up. "When I decided to stay with horses, I learned a lot about them because I couldn't find anyone who really knew much about them."

Cinching Up Self-Esteem

Wyllie says that the role of the horse has changed a good deal over the last hundred years. "After 1900, the focus shifted to recreation and sports." Things are changing again in the new millennium. "Now the horse is training people in the way liberal arts colleges once did, first and most importantly, in how to communicate. Secondly, how to get results which increase self-worth and leadership skills."

Horses' new role is as a mental and emotional asset, says Wyllie. He has honed his programs to accomplish that with horses.

"When you believe in yourself you can deal with authority," he remarks. "That's what you have to do with the horse, believe in yourself."

Today, like most days, Wyllie pulls into the barn on Kanan Road halfway between the Malibu coast and Agoura Hills, with an eye to the horizon, skimming the rocky hilltops close by. There are more months of golden fire-prone brush than green foliage here. Ten horses sound a welcome in unison—from the bright speckled Appaloosa, Spot, to the chestnut Arabian, Tony, all acknowledge his arrival.

"Horses mean a lot of things to me. Actually they're my closest companions. I spend so much time with them that I have taken on a lot of the qualities that they have—live for the moment, make a decision immediately—all things that I use," Wyllie reflects. "One of the great things about the job I have is lots of soul time. When I'm teaching, particularly on the trail, there's a lot of time for thinking and observing."

∩ Try This

If you've never been around horses, start by visiting a local tack shop if one is accessible in your area. Talk to the staff and ask for advice; one of the best ways to learn about the local horse scene is word-of-mouth. Most horse people gladly offer advice. Ask about college riding programs in your area—many also offer reasonably priced community programs and are especially well-suited for beginners. Good basics are essential. Look for small class sizes, but not necessarily private lessons to start. It helps to have another student to watch.

If you're an experienced equestrian, grab some paper. Jot down five ways the horse has enhanced your awareness of the moment or ability to be present. (Or, when you ignored the occasion and hit the ground.)

Chapter Two

Power
. . . truths of the fast track

*The highest type of ruler is one of whose existence the
people are barely aware.*

—Lao Tzu, translated by John C.H. Wu

NO ONE KNOWS THE MEANING OF POWER QUITE LIKE JOCKEYS,
whose profession requires that they negotiate with another
species at speeds of thirty-five to forty miles per hour. Among
the world's fittest athletes, what jockeys learn on the back of a
horse illuminates the essence of power.

"How can I be like 102 pounds and on constant good
terms with Thoroughbred racehorses that weigh 1,200 pounds
when they're trained for speed and energy? Yet, the lightest

touch of a rein, or dropping your heel, or a simple 'Whoa' will slow them down, or make them relax. You wonder, why do they allow us to do that?" reflects jockey Julie Krone, the only woman inducted into Thoroughbred Racing's Hall of Fame. Barely missing a beat she explains, "It's done through communication—giving and taking—developing a rapport with a horse. They're so subtle."

The Dance of (Horse) Power

With more than 21,000 career rides logged by her twentieth year of competition in a sport traditionally dominated by men, the 4'10½" jockey demonstrated an equine dance of power to the tune of more than $84 million in purse winnings by the end of 2003. "Thoroughbreds are unique compared to many other horses. They take things more seriously. When you give and take with a Thoroughbred, it's amplified," notes Krone.

Born Julieann (*Daily Racing Form* listed her name as Julie the first time she raced and it stuck), Krone took off in the first phase of a groundbreaking career in 1981, becoming a household name as she racked up 3,545 wins, including the Belmont Stakes aboard Colonial Affair in 1993 (the first Triple Crown race won by a female jockey) before retiring in 1999 at age thirty-five, the year her mother died of cancer. After a three-and-a-half-year hiatus, the petite blonde resumed racing in 2002, winning twenty races and three stakes events her first two months back in the saddle. Another landmark was etched when Krone streaked across the wire aboard Candy Ride in the

2003 Pacific Classic at Del Mar, California, becoming the first female jockey to win a million-dollar race. (And, she did it at the age of forty.)

Krone also made history when she became the first female rider to win a Breeder's Cup race aboard Unbridled. "It's absolutely the most fun you can have," remembers Krone. Still, an element of performance and constant vigilance are imperative for the job, she insists.

Jockeys must attune to nature's most literal horse power in a matter of minutes to even make it around the track. A typical day at work is synonymous with repeatedly jumping off one mount and climbing aboard the next.

"They surprise you because they're so individual. Some of them enjoy it when you give them boundaries, like 'Naaah, don't do that,' and they're like, 'OK, thank you for keeping my brain together!' Others are very distant and capable on their own and all you get to do is enjoy them," says Krone, who moved from her East Coast roots to California during her time away from competition. "You always are adjusting to the horses. They're a lot like people. I appreciate them more and more as I get older. I really think that they have spirits and they are very capable of a lot of communication."

Power in Possibilities

Born in Eau Claire, Michigan, in the southwest corner of the state, Krone's early life was defined by moments with horses. "I can take myself back to being a kid and meeting my friends at midnight to TP somebody's house on horseback," describes Krone. "I remember one night—I'm bareback on my pony, shorts, barefoot, tan from summer with little wear marks on the back of the calf where the horse sweats and hair sticks to your legs. My pony was grazing and I had a plastic bag full of toilet paper. We had this waiting spot. I remember lying on my pony's back and swatting off mosquitoes. The spring peepers were going and the moon was as full as it could be. You could just see everything. I was only nine or ten, but I remember thinking, I will never forget this moment in my whole life."

Taught to ride by her mother Judi Krone, a dressage rider and all-around horse trainer—the budding jockey's equestrian education was diverse. As a child, she drove a cart and a buggy, was champion in trail (riding), and was a Green Champion Pony Hunter. "I was Green Champion Goat Showman—not that a goat has anything to do with a horse," she laughs.

However, it was a clinic on haute-école (French for high school) horse training that Krone describes as teaching her "the most incredible thing I learned growing up." She learned to train horses to kneel, bow, sit down, lie down, nod yes and no, climb aboard a teeter-totter, and assorted other tricks. "You did it all with nothing on the horse, not a speck of tack!" she exclaims. "All from just giving, taking, and rewarding."

Significantly, the late Chuck Grant who taught the clinic (a master of many riding disciplines and considered the "Father of American Dressage"), accurately predicted Krone's future as a "fine race rider" before she ever sat on a racehorse, in a book inscription to her mother.

"I was maybe one of the youngest people ever allowed in one of his clinics and I never got to assume that a horse was not capable of that level of intelligence. I think to this day, that is what makes a difference with me and the Thoroughbreds," she adds.

Krone is adamant about the importance of well-rounded horse people who make a point of learning every riding style. "I'm very offended by riding style snobs," she remarks. In the horse world, like the world in general, different routes to knowledge or power often share more commonalities than differences, if you're willing to distill the essence.

A Tad of Tolerance

"One of Charlie Whittingham's things was, 'Just pay attention!'" says Krone remembering the sharp tongue and quick wit of racing's legendary Hall of Fame trainer (who died in 1999). "I think horses are very tolerant. We miss so much of what they are trying to communicate. In a herd, if one looks at another and flicks an ear, or swishes a tail, or moves a certain way, other horses notice it," reflects Krone, whose racing career has taken her from Sweden to Japan, where she was the first woman to ride and win at Tokyo Race Course. "If they're sad or upset, I think they can really live within themselves."

Some horses are bursting with expression. "They're so aware of the people around them and they interact," she explains. "Like when someone reaches up to sponge their head and give them a bath, they drop their head down and flip their little lips and the soap goes everywhere. Those are the horses that are so fun to be around."

The Role of Respect

The word "respect" surfaces repeatedly in conversation with Krone about horses. "The core of Lao Tzu's written philosophy deals with the art of getting out of one's own way, learning how to act without forcing conclusions, and living in skillful harmony with the processes of nature instead of trying to push them around," wrote Alan Watts in the book *What Is Tao?** Applying such principles to horses is what jockeys do daily.

"Horses feel the energy and the people watching them," says Krone. Jockeys are likewise acutely aware of their surroundings, amidst intense posttime concentration. "It's fun when you ride by and the person goes, 'Oh, I like the way that one looks!' Or, the horse will sneeze, bounce around, and arch its neck or something, and people are actually amazed by it."

Inducted into the Cowgirl Hall of Fame in Forth Worth, Texas in 1999, Krone joined a lineup of American icons such as Annie Oakley, Dale Evans, and Patsy Cline. "There are horses that I've become such good friends with that I know what they're thinking. They feel like family members, or just an extension of me," remarks Krone.

"It's a lot like life. You can be in a family environment and everyone is always there and as you get a little bit older—grandparents die. Sometimes I see horses [around the track] that raced

*Copyright © 2000 by Mark Watts. Reprinted with permission of New World Library, Novato, CA. *www.newworldlibrary.com* or 800-972-6657 ext 52.

for years. You get a relationship with them. As my life advanced with racehorses, I had to learn how to be a little detached at times." But every time she's even contemplated another career, Krone found it impossible to give up horses. "They always keep dragging me back." The truth is an existence; the horse is her path.

Horses and Humility

Jockey Gary Stevens doesn't hesitate to look you straight in the eye and say it like it is. "It doesn't matter what I've done in my past. Every ride, I'm constantly trying to prove myself. That's what keeps us humble. The power factor is not really there. Like an actor's only as good as his last movie, I'm only as good as my last ride." A Hall of Fame jockey with six Triple Crown racing victories (three in the Kentucky Derby), a Dubai World Cup title, eight Breeders' Cup race firsts, and more than 4,500 total wins to his credit before he turned forty, three months after that birthday Stevens made a noteworthy acting debut as jockey George Woolf in the movie "Seabiscuit." Less than a month after the film premiere, he was almost killed in a riding accident at the finish of the Arlington Million in Chicago. After a short, intense recovery Stevens climbed back in the saddle a few weeks later, and started racing again.

"I believe there is some kind of sixth sense between human and animal. That horse knows that I want to win every race I go out in. Somehow, I'm able to get that feeling through to the horse. If they don't have the same competitive attitude as I have, then I'm not the right rider for them."

Born in Boise, Idaho, Stevens learned to ride about the time he learned to walk. His mother was a Rodeo Queen and barrel racer; his father trained horses first as a hobby, then a profession. But Stevens's path to horses wasn't entirely smooth. He took a bad spill as a child off a horse, got scared, and essentially lost interest. At six, a degenerative hip ailment put young Stevens's leg in a full-length steel brace for eighteen months. "When you're that age, kids can be very, very cruel," he recalls. "It made me tough and want to succeed in everything I do. I learned to ride a bike with one leg and started playing drums." (Stevens, in fact, still plays the drums.)

Had it not been for his elder brother Scott, Stevens's career path might have been drastically different. "My brother started riding and I always tried to follow in his footsteps. I galloped my first racehorse when I was eleven," he recalls. "I felt the power and just fell in love with it, right then. That was it!" At fourteen, Stevens rode his first races at some small tracks in Utah. He left home in 1979 at sixteen and rode his first professional horse race at an age when most teens are jockeying for driver's licenses. Stevens's real-life mounts had earned more than $187 million in purses by the time film fans saw the budding actor in "Seabiscuit" the summer of 2003.

Yin, Yang of Power

A constant awareness of life's fragility is never far from the muscles, horse power, and speed. "I think Charlie Whittingham said it best, that 'Horses are like strawberries. They can spoil overnight,'" comments Stevens. "One misstep and it's over. It's the same for us as jockeys."

Stevens retired briefly from racing in 1999, due to knee problems. "I went to the vortexes in Sedona, Arizona, and just tried to get an answer of what I was supposed to do. It was five days after I retired," he remembers. "For whatever reason, the answer I left there with was that I was going to ride again and that's what I was supposed to do." Ten months later, Stevens indeed returned to racing at the top of the game.

Part Iroquois on his father's side, an eagle tattoo with blood drops for each Kentucky Derby win, flies on the jockey's right shoulder, hidden beneath racing silks. On Stevens's left shoulder, a tattooed young Native American brave reaches his hands out for the eagle to land. "Every time I go into a big race I feel like I'm preparing for battle and I take no prisoners," he remarks. "I'm very passionate about our sport. I love nothing better than riding a long shot in a big race and winning," says five-foot-four-inch Stevens, whose eyes are as blue as the sky.

A collector of Native American and Western art, Stevens cites his favorite all-time mount (coincidentally) as Silver Charm—the gray stallion he rode to win the 1997 Kentucky Derby. "The reason is, he just had such a huge heart. He was a horse who hated to lose. He won so many close races," recalls Stevens. "I think he was a little bit of an overachiever. He wasn't supposed to be as good as what he turned out to be." (Silver Charm also won the Dubai World Cup with Stevens—a $6 million purse that year.)

It's a sunny March afternoon at Santa Anita racetrack in Arcadia, California as Stevens sips a cup of coffee in the jock's kitchen during a break between races. He's just been asked for thoughts about what makes a winning mount. "You've got to have a horse that's an athlete physically. Then, that horse has got to be nurtured from the time he's a baby to be able to develop— given the best feeds there are and just looked after. They're just like an infant child," explains Stevens, himself a father of four.

"They need love, they need care, and then they need to be trained in the right way. When I say the right way, to me that means for a horse to be relaxed and able to use the athletic abilities he was born with. The desire to run is bred into the good Thoroughbreds. It's in their genes. You don't have to teach them competitiveness. It's either there, or it's not."

☾ TRY THIS

Spend a day at the races. A general admission ticket will get you an up-close view of the jockeys and horse power in front of you. Get close enough to hear the thunder of hooves and see the turf fly. Be sure to visit the paddock before each race, and take a notebook. (Hint: wear comfortable walking shoes.) Pay attention to a single jockey throughout the day and observe how much time is actually available to get in sync with a new mount before heading onto the track. Each time the jockey saddles up, jot down a word or phrase that describes your observations about the rider or horse. At the end of the day, see how your notes might apply to a power-related issue in your life. (Want more on racing? Visit National Thoroughbred Racing Association's Web site: *www.ntra.com*.)

Chapter Three

Trust
. . . trotting toward a different reality

Training is really more under-
standing the animal than anything
else. It is also a profession that if
you're going to be very good, or a
master, it has to be in your blood or
your mind . . .

—Corky Randall

SOME OF HOLLYWOOD'S BIGGEST CELEBRITIES BET THEIR LIVES ON the trust between movie horses and their trainers when they saddle up for a role. Like conductors leading an orchestra, trainers cue equine thespians to rear, nod, give horse smiles, and paw, with a move of an arm or the point of a hand—all invisible to the camera's eye. And, if the horse shared his perspective (hey—this is Hollywood!), he might say, "Trust can break through the barriers of mere appearances."

Leap of Faith: Take One

A galloping black Friesian gelding burst through two door-sized sheets of paper covering the end of the barn—held together like a pseudo "wall" with masking tape. Legendary Hollywood horse trainer Corky Randall surveyed the training progress of Fedde, a mount destined for star Antonio Banderas to ride in the 1998 blockbuster film *The Mask of Zorro*.

"You've got to encourage them little by little, make them trust you and the fact that it will always break away," explains Randall. "And it does. Otherwise, you can say goodbye to three months of training."

Fedde first got comfortable moving through paper positioned with a visible gap in between (a feat in itself for many horses). The pieces were slowly moved closer together during the course of several months.

By the time film production began in Mexico, Fedde's trust and training were firmly in place. Had a personal growth seminar camped out on set, the horse could have demonstrated some lessons on breaking the boundaries of perception. (Going through solid-looking surfaces is not among the repertoire of typical horse behaviors.) Besides making an equine leap of faith, Fedde showed how trust turned a one-time Dutch farmer's horse into a half-ton movie star—in a manner of speaking.

"All animals have to have a trust in their trainers. That's how they accomplish getting the animal to do what they would like it to do—because that animal learns to trust that person," explains Randall, whose father the late Glenn Randall Sr., trained Roy Rogers's Trigger and even housebroke the horse. "They also depend on people to keep them out of trouble."

One of four horses portraying Zorro's equine sidekick, Tornado, Fedde put in an Oscar-worthy performance in several memorable scenes. The thick-maned horse barreled through an army barracks' "wall" (a Styrofoam version in the movie), galloped up a flight of stairs, and even raised his upper lip in a sneaky smile on cue, as Zorro hit the ground instead of the saddle, after jumping from a roof.

"The whole thing is, you have to be able to bring an animal with the right frame of mind, to the right place, and the right actor. You have to have the ability to find the horse first off, know the horse, and know where the animal fits in the picture—where he will do his best job," explains Randall, now retired. "You also have to realize there will be days that you think he'd be great and he won't do anything. That's when you've got to reach back there and get another one. You never know which one may save your life that day."

Central Casting: Horse Shaman

Rarely without baseball cap, jeans, and a wad of chewing tobacco, Randall's humble demeanor belies his stature as an international role model. A two-time winner of the Patsy Award (the animal trainer's Oscar) and recipient of the Humanitarian Award from the Society for the Prevention of Cruelty to Animals Los Angeles in 1982, Randall's efforts furthered legislation safeguarding animals. "The training of animals has come a long way from when I first came around movies," he reflects.

Even now, as horses roam only the walls in photographs at the once-bustling Randall Ranch outside Los Angeles, this sage of Hollywood horse training has been nominated for a star on Hollywood's Walk of Fame by filmmaker friends and fans for all he represents.

Born in 1929 in Gering, Nebraska, the second-generation of what would become a horse-training dynasty, Randall was diagnosed with polio as a young boy. "In Lincoln, Nebraska, the hospital for kids with polio was putting spikes in the bone to try to stretch the bone out. My dad wouldn't allow it, so they took me home and my grandmother rubbed my legs and exercised them. I jumped rope and did exercises," he remembers. By age "nine or ten" Randall was galloping Thoroughbred colts in the morning for his father before going to school.

"Riding a horse made me equal with anybody. On the ground, I couldn't run as fast as other people. I couldn't do a lot of things that other people with two good legs could do. Once I got on a horse, then everything was equal."

Randall first sampled the film business at Republic Studios during high school and never contemplated another lifestyle. "When I got to the studios and wrangled horses, I thought that was the greatest thing ever." From his first major assignment on *The Alamo*, Randall's five-decade career in Hollywood included dozens of feature films and television shows, from *How the West Was Won*, *Soldier Blue*, and *The Misfits* (Clark Gable stood out among countless stars he's worked with), to *Buffalo Girls*, *Hot to Trot*, and *Indiana Jones and the Last Crusade*. His film credits are loaded with television classics like *Spin & Marty* and the *Zorro* TV series.

However, it was the beloved Walter Farley novel-turned-movie *The Black Stallion* that established Randall's training legacy in his own right, proving beyond a doubt horses were in his blood and mind. An extraordinary production, with some of the most challenging horse scenes ever filmed, Randall cites the black Arabian stallion star—whose real name was Cass-olé—as his all-time favorite equine actor.

"He was so smart and such a character. Cass-olé loved to be around people and he loved to make pictures," recalls Randall. "He was almost human. He even had an expression on his face and horses usually don't have expressions." Randall describes a photograph that captured one particularly bad day of filming. "I've got a mean look on my face and right over my shoulder is Cass-olé, and he's looking just like that, too. It looked like if we could get to you, we were going to eat you up."

Sometimes, he notes, humans and horses are remarkably similar. "You run into exceptional animals. They come like people, some are just outstandingly brilliant in certain fields. Cass-olé was an exception, as was the bay horse we used in *Hot to Trot*. They're kind of like little kids; they like to show off and they're just very easy to work in a picture. They seem like a well-trained actor, they just fall in there and do their part." Randall finishes the story eager to get outside; the temperature is rising and his garden needs watering. "Others, like some people, don't put in that little extra pizzazz. These two horses went to the heights."

Sprouting Wings

Outdoors past the tomato plants, in an arena Randall still grooms with his tractor, is the spot where the TriStar film label's animated feature logo Pegasus was filmed. For years the winged horse, played by a white Arabian gelding named T-Bone, introduced TriStar productions on screen. (Columbia TriStar Motion Picture Group is now part of Sony Entertainment.) T-Bone had successfully worked for Randall in *Return of the Black Stallion* (the sequel to *The Black Stallion*) as a female (horse) love interest.

The Pegasus sequence was filmed at night in an L-shaped alley that was constructed in the arena with black curtain sides twenty feet tall. T-Bone got a powder job to appear even whiter. "He looked like a ghost," recalls Randall. Positioned at one end of the arena, T-Bone was turned loose when Randall called. Galloping down the passage, and around the corner, the horse leaped a jump at the end to reach his trainer. Movie buffs will note, in the oldest versions of the TriStar's animated feature logo, the Pegasus gets his wings the moment he jumps. What an apt analogy for matters of trust.

"I think there are still a lot of successful pictures to be made with horses, if you can capture the relationship between the animal and the person," remarks Randall. "Like they did in

The Black Stallion. What's beautiful about the story is it's mystical, make believe. A young boy with this great stallion, on an island, having this great adventure. Kind of like Robinson Crusoe." Sometimes real life can be as much of an adventure as fantasy.

Right Place, Right Time

At an age when most boys are playing video games and riding skateboards, Matt Zoppe does what his family has done for four generations. From atop his brother's shoulders, on top of an 1,800-pound stallion in motion, he propels himself into a backward somersault through the air. He lands upright on a second horse following closely behind, and the audience erupts with applause.

"When you hit that horse's back and you land it for the first time, it's a feeling and a half, let me tell you. It goes through you like electricity. Your heart will jump into your throat, your stomach, bounce all around your body," describes Zoppe. He first performed the horse-to-horse somersault at fourteen, while then touring with the Tarzan Zerbini Circus with his family. "I was the youngest person that I know of who has ever done that trick in the world. I was very proud of that," Zoppe says.

Now twenty, with a dark mane of hair and smoldering looks, Zoppe is intent on mastering an even more difficult maneuver called the "full twist." "There's only a handful of people who have done that trick from one horse to another," he notes. Two such individuals are his uncles, Zoppe adds.

"You've got to have trust in your animals," he explains. "You've got to be on the ball all the time, right at that moment. I've been on some horses I did not trust and I was like a wired-up cat—you have to be. When you've got a new horse underneath your feet, or behind you and you're going to land on them, you'd better be on the ball." Anyone who's contemplated truths about being at the right place at the right time could find Zoppe the ultimate illustration. Right place, right time? "Now that's what I mean!"

A fourth-generation bareback rider, with a heritage of two great circus families, both his mother's side (the Zamperla family) and father's (the Zoppe's) have been in show business for seven generations. "I guess you could say I was bred into it," says the lithe young man whose 5'7"-inch frame appears engineered for the spotlight. At the family home in Florida, a wall is devoted to photographs of family members doing horse-to-horse tricks. "I'm going to be up there with a somersault and a full twist," Zoppe promises. "It's really cool. All my uncles and my cousins—everybody is there."

The performer has logged thousands of miles on tour since childhood, sometimes in acts with one, or all, of his three brothers. After crisscrossing the United States and Canada with "Cheval" ("Horse"), performing throughout the show's entire two-year run, Zoppe took on a starring role at Orlando's Arabian Nights equestrian attraction in 2003. "I think God gave me a gift. Everybody has their gift and it's mine to work with horses. We understand each other pretty good," remarks Zoppe. With horses, understanding is more than a concept.

"There's a vibe you get from a horse. I've had horses that when I first put them in the show, I completely trusted them. I didn't have to think twice. There was just a connection. But then you get horses that have been handled a little bit and go through a couple of hands before they get to you. Those are the ones you kind of watch out for. They're good horses, they just need somebody that can understand them. But in the beginning, you've got to be really, really aware. Many things can go wrong and you can get hurt big time." The immediacy involved in working with horses allows for no lapse in consciousness. Yet, like any path embraced as a way of life, horses bring the ebb and flow of experiences.

The Constant in Change

"They'll surprise you forever. Through the good times and bad times, things don't change between you and your animal. You treat them good, like you should, things don't change and you can always count on them. You always have somebody to go to. I say 'somebody' like it's a person. That's what they are to me," reflects Zoppe in a contemplative moment.

Cognac, a Percheron stallion Zoppe bought as an unbroken two-year-old in Canada, comes across as an equine soul mate. "I can get very emotional sometimes and can't talk to anybody. I just go out there and sit on him bareback while he walks around. That's my therapy right there. He lets me lay on his back and think." Now six, Cognac's back is 5'8" above the ground.

Zoppe first spotted Cognac in a field of draft horses while driving along a country road two hours north of Quebec City, with his brother while they were on tour. "He'd never had anybody on his back—I was the first person. I was the first person to ever do a somersault on him. That's special for a horse to allow you. They trust you, as you trust them. The way he performs for me, it's like he was put on this earth for bareback riding and I found him."

In a multitude of ways, horses have always been a part of Zoppe's extended family. "Ever since I can remember, I could always escape and go see my horses, even when I was little, five, six, seven years old. I think it kept me out of trouble that most kids get into when they don't have something like that around. I was just so in love and fascinated by them. If there's a movie with a horse in it, I will go see it, just for the horse."

Not surprisingly, even vacations from touring and performances tend to be horse-oriented. "I can't get away from them, no matter what. If I went to Mexico, I'd probably find a nice stable and ride horses on the beach. If I had enough time, I would go home and practice with my younger brothers on their horses." Zoppe fondly recalls a trip to his cousin's circus school in France. "It's every bareback rider's dream to travel from country to country to ride."

He admits, the prospect of Hollywood and riding in films holds a personal intrigue, as do continuing challenges of bareback riding arts, like mastering the full twist horse-to-horse. "When I see an artist or performer do something that just totally blows my mind, I picture myself being that person, doing that trick," says Zoppe. "I hope I give that feeling to other people, too."

Today, Zoppe will perform in two shows back-to-back, challenged each time to align mind, body, and soul together with his massive equine companion. "It's pretty amazing what a horse can do to your life and how it can turn it around and make it so much better," he reflects. "A lot of people don't know about horses and how they can help you get through life. It would surprise them if they were to take some time out and get to know one." Zoppe heads off toward makeup. It's time to change out of his street clothes. One more thought occurs to him, "I couldn't see my life without them, I really couldn't."

☊ TRY THIS

How would you feel about literally running through a "wall" of paper? Would you trust someone enough to believe there was nothing behind it? Whether the thought is exhilarating or terrifying, it's food for self-reflection. Learn something about how horses and other animal actors are protected in film and television by visiting the American Humane Association Film and TV Unit's Web site at *www.ahafilm.org*. Click on "Animal Film Reviews" to get the scoop on what happens behind-the-scenes. Visualize yourself doing a backward somersault and landing on your feet atop a moving horse in the glare of a spotlight, while 2,000 people wildly applaud.

Chapter Four

Healing
. . . horse medicine 101

You could just sit with a horse and
feel better . . .

—Michael McMeel

INSIDE CENTRAL JUVENILE HALL IN
downtown Los Angeles, near a tangle
of freeways and cement, Inner City
Slickers has set up camp for the day. Horse trailers roll through
gates topped by concertina wire and deposit their four-legged
occupants inside. A cowboy-hat-clad contingent of rodeo professionals, Hollywood stunt men, and assorted horse lovers—all
volunteers—have already positioned hay bales, water buckets, and
paraphernalia in one corner of the rectangular grass field. They
have teamed up with mounts, while founder Michael McMeel
chats with a "Juvy Hall" staff member, who may get a surprise
ride before the day is over.

A door swings open and forty-some youngsters march out single file, wrists together behind their backs. Some have been charged with theft, drug dealing, rape, and even murder. Some were too difficult for their parents to handle and enough truancy and broken laws added up. In the next fifteen minutes, the multi-racial collection of eight-to-twenty-one-year-olds will be split into "posses" and find horse brushes and hoof picks thrust in their hands. As they grapple with climbing into a saddle for the first time, even tough gang members with hardened facial expressions crack a smile—and some giggle. For the next few hours they will be kids having fun, and the horses don't know or care what they're in for.

Rx: Old West

"I had no idea ten years ago that I'd be living on a ranch doing this," says McMeel, who was a drummer for the rock 'n roll group Three Dog Night in a former career. "I have a whole closet of Armani suits I never wear anymore. I'm just in jeans, cowboy hat, whatever." Inspired by the film *City Slickers*, McMeel came up with the idea of developing an Old West program involving horses for inner-city kids in 1994. He'd already begun developing programs for "at risk" youth through The Awareness Foundation, a charity he began two years earlier, after watching fires raging in the city during the Los Angeles riots, from an office in Hollywood. The idea was born while McMeel was shooting a commercial at a site near Agua Dulce, California, which is now home to the Inner City Slickers Ranch.

With an OK from Castle Rock Entertainment to use the name, Inner City Slickers galloped into existence with neither horses nor ranch. McMeel and some horse-savvy friends rented both. He formed a new nonprofit with the tagline, "Where The Cowboys Meet the Street Boys," and brought out forty kids for the first event.

"I really didn't know the impact it would have until we actually did it," recalls McMeel, whose own horse skills were pretty rusty at the first Inner City Slickers event. He rode when he was growing up in Colorado, but when he went into music had given it up. "I didn't have much of a curriculum at the time. I just knew I wanted to have kids be on horses, touch horses, groom them, and take care of them. The results were just astounding. They're struck with awe, like 'Oh my God, look at this horse!' and then they're struck with fear. If the horse sneezes on you, it's like, 'Oooh.'" Many youngsters arrived in their best tennis shoes and didn't want to get dirty. "We did it for three days and it was astonishing, just in regard to character building," says McMeel.

He estimates 7,000 or more "at risk" youth have participated in Inner City Slickers so far. Many ongoing activities are at the ranch, which is thirty-five miles and a world away from downtown Los Angeles. Often such an event marks the first time many children have traveled outside the inner city.

A Horse a Day Takes the Garbage Away

"A lot of kids that I run into, their character is out the bottom. They're closed off; they don't really want to participate; they'll hang out with their clique; they're disrespectful, and not kind to each other," explains McMeel, on a day when temperatures soar above 100 degrees at the ranch. A warm breeze keeps the wind chimes in a nearby tree softly tinkling. "Horses just completely cut across any of your bullshit. Whatever it might be, it just neutralizes and you get to see the real person in front of you. You get to see how they really react and how they respond. That's half the battle as far as trying to work with people—to get them off this attitude thing. You want to get to that individual in there and the horse just does it."

McMeel's face comes to life as he recalls the day Wilbur, a gray Arabian, brought added excitement to an Inner City Slickers event at Camp Scudder, a Los Angeles juvenile detention center. "Wilbur can be a little spirited and this girl gets on him. We work out in the soccer field there. So she's walking and trotting and all the sudden he's moving a little bit quicker and she screams—and he takes off. So Wilbur is going around the soccer field, once, twice. Every time he comes close to the kids, everybody screams, and he goes faster, but she's holding on. Finally, we get him; she climbs off almost hysterical; yet, it was almost thrilling for her. We reiterated again, 'You can't scream around the horses,' and as a joke I said, 'OK, who wants to ride Wilbur now?' and everybody raised their hands. That girl got on again. It was really a shot in the arm as far as her own character, having the courage to push through the fear and get back on the horse and ride him."

Another story comes to mind—the 250-pound gang member who started crying when he was heaved aboard a steady Appaloosa mare named Mariposa. "He was afraid of getting hurt," recalls McMeel. He went "from this tough 'Screw you' kind of guy, to 'Oh, please help!'"

On a personal level, a chestnut Thoroughbred gelding named Max (aka Maximillion), whom McMeel bought as a three-year-old from one of his wranglers, proved to be a significant force in the development of Inner City Slickers. "Max was too much of a horse for me when I got him," remembers McMeel. "I had just gotten back into horses, so here's this one who basically bucks me off a cliff, kicks me in the knee—and just missed shattering it—stepped on my toe, and took my toenail off. I mean, it was two months of amazing crap and I had a fear of this horse because I kept getting hurt. But I continued with him."

McMeel points to a dramatic horse head sculpture on a shelf that reminds him of Max. He will never sell the horse; Max means too much. "He was really the impetus for getting me as involved with Slickers as I am now. Isn't that funny? He was just kind of the cornerstone. He ignited something in me that helped me create this entire thing."

Now surveying ten acres of horse corrals, barns, facilities, and animals, in contrast to the spotlights and applause known during a million miles of touring with Three Dog Night, it could be said that life is emulating art—in a manner of speaking. McMeel remembers the song "Try a little Tenderness" written by Otis Redding, as his favorite of the many played with the band. Little could he have envisioned then, how prophetic the title would become for his future work and life.

When Inner City Slickers acquired its own ranch several years into its existence, McMeel, his daughter Amber, and fiancé

Erlida, (now wife) moved from a two-bedroom apartment in the San Fernando Valley to the marginally developed property. "It was overwhelming when we came out here," recalls McMeel. "Now it's too small. I've built on everything I can." An Old West town made by volunteers resembles a Western movie set, although the general store, soda saloon, hotel, jail, and old-time photographer's studio reveal bunk beds behind the facades.

"We're definitely not trying to turn kids into cowboys, but we are definitely wanting them to have new experiences, memories that they can take with them." Tan from days in the sun, McMeel reflects, "Horses have a way of making the kids courageous."

Galloping Through the Prejudice Gulch

In the ten years since Slickers began, McMeel and his posse of volunteer staff have honed the program to build confidence, character, self-esteem, break down social prejudices, and prevent the type of beliefs and behavior that land kids in Juvenile Hall or worse. An ever-widening range of participants include community groups, schools, churches, and law enforcement agencies—from Mother's Against Gangs to the Agape International Center of Truth, to the Asian Crime Task Force and even Volunteers of America. McMeel is contemplating taking the Slickers program nationwide. "I'd definitely like to have a Slickers in every major metropolitan area," he says. Northern California has participated in the activities for a number of years.

"The thing I like about the concept of a cowboy is that there's just something that goes along with it—someone that's dependable, kind, and somebody that gives a darn. It has connected so many wonderful attributes for me," says McMeel, who spent eight months walking the streets of South Central and East Los Angeles after the riots to understand the inner city's problems better, often stopping in the churches. "That's where the people were." An initial plan to develop a television series about the inner city was shelved when McMeel's Awareness Foundation began. By the time Billy Crystal and the *City Slickers* film rode on the horizon, McMeel had successfully implemented a number of projects already dealing with racial and cultural issues.

"We've designed this program to be challenging, to really push the envelope. We tell them they're going to learn to take care of a horse, control a horse. We talk a lot about respect—for this animal and its capabilities, like its strength, its power, its quickness. You can't muscle a horse." The point hits home as the youngsters learn to pick up a hoof and bridle a horse, some more successfully than others. "It really makes them think outside their box, because they have a particular way of thinking," McMeel reflects. Care of the horses, watering, and feeding—particular eye-openers for inner city kids—aren't just chores, but responsibility. "It's not like the horses are running wild in the mountains," McMeel reminds each group of Slickers. "If we forget to help them they will perish."

The thrill of learning to ride is balanced with doses of shoveling horse manure. "A lot of the kids don't realize how important it is to be able to work as a team. In fact, most of them don't work as a team very well at all." McMeel delightedly describes some of the team-building activities Slickers are exposed to—for instance, the "Wall of Hay," a fifteen-foot tall challenge course-type obstacle. Not to be forgotten are the cattle drives on foot while the horses take a siesta in their stalls.

Many of the ongoing activities at the Slickers Ranch include overnights, with campfires as a part of the ritual. As firewood crackles and horses whinny in the distance, kids who have never heard the wild yodels of coyotes at night are disclosing private thoughts. "We talk about prejudice, about prejudging. That's what prejudice is. As soon as I walk in the door, you're going to prejudge who I am. It comes with the territory," notes McMeel. "You meet a person on the street and you have a certain concept of who they are. You meet a horse, or an animal, and you have a preconceived idea of who they are. Then you actually start working with that individual, horse or person, and you say, 'Gee, it isn't that way at all.'"

McMeel describes another fireside tradition that caps the day-long activities. "We do this thing from the *City Slickers* movie where they talk about 'what's your best day and what's your unhappiest?' One kid said the worst day was when he walked into the bathroom and saw his younger brother had hung himself. He cut him down and it saved his life. So, it turned out to be one of the happiest days of his life, too." McMeel reflects, "Sharing something personal is probably the toughest thing about Inner City Slickers. There is a kind of uniting that takes place on that night—a new level of intimacy that's been reached with the kids and the adults." McMeel explains more, "That's the whole thing with being prejudiced and looking at people in a way that's not

OK. Bottom line is we just all have the same stuff going on. We're all afraid; we're trying to be the best we can."

Inner City Slickers has a motto, "May they never be the same." Watching McMeel hop in a dusty truck and make the rounds past the pipe corrals below leaves no doubt the words might well fit him. "If you ride a horse, there are times you're going to fall off and I've had my share of that," he remarks, looking more like a man of the earth than a former rock 'n' roll star. "I don't have to ride all the time. I just like being around the horses. I like taking care of them. Just this morning when I was mowing the lawn, I saw two people riding down the road and I just stopped. I just love seeing people on horses. It signifies there's a freedom there. I really cannot even articulate what it is. I notice it all the time when I see a horse and person out riding. It just is a boost for me."

The Heart Part

One of the greatest accomplishments of the twentieth century's holistic health personal growth movement was to popularize concepts of the mind-body-soul connection to such a degree that when the new millennium began, you could discuss "energy" or matters like animal-related therapy in a mainstream setting and people generally would have some familiarity with the concepts. The North American Riding for the Handicapped Association (NARHA) is a clearing-house of information and contacts for therapeutic riding programs, plus countless success stories.

Sometimes, the relationship between horse and human proves a medicine so strong it happens on its own.

Octavio Munguia brims with good looks, charm, and an electric smile that intensifies the innate grace of an accomplished Mexican hotelier. Munguia grabs his cane and rises to his feet, heading to the parking lot in a twisting, yet steady gait. The manager at the small, pricey La Cienega Boulevard restaurant in Los Angeles is clearly eager to close for the night and go home. The open-late Coffee Bean & Tea Leaf on Robertson Boulevard will make do to finish a conversation about a well-bred horse in Utah that Munguia may take home to Puerto Vallarta, Mexico, where he lives at the ocean's edge at his Los Tules Resort hotel operation.

"I didn't realize how much horses were part of my life until I didn't ride," remarks Munguia, who is temporarily horseless for the first time in years. He clarifies, "I've been without a horse but I've not been apart from the horse world. I've gotten involved with polo a lot." Munguia sponsors a talented young player some twenty years his junior. Polo season in Careyes, about 100 miles south of "Vallarta," runs from November to April, drawing many from the international polo set. "Careyes is a very, very special place," notes Munguia, who makes the jaunt regularly to attend the games. "Less than half a mile from the beach, you have these two regulation polo fields of perfectly level grass surrounded by this tropical jungle. The town itself is a small, nice town, but the homes—every home is like a dream. It's one of the best-kept secrets. I'm very proud because it's Mexico and you see all these people from Europe and the States coming here going, 'Wow!'"

Munguia's eyes sparkle, "It's horse heaven for people who love polo or riding. You can ride on the beach, on the trails, and see the polo games." He pauses a moment, thinking out loud, "In a way, it's a world of money, but we don't look at it that way, we just look at it as a world of horses and what they do and the satisfaction they bring."

Early Impressions

The son of a Mexican filmmaker, Munguia grew up with generous exposure to film and television while a boy in Mexico City. Several in particular, sparked early fantasies about horses. "I think most kids envision themselves as Zorro or the Lone Ranger," Munguia laughs. "I used to watch them all the time. To get on a horse and take off, you own the world, right?"

His uncle's rancho, an ancient Mexican hacienda several hours north of the city in the state of Hidalgo, gave Munguia a first exposure to horses that imitated his favorite TV shows. "At that time, I'm talking early 1960s, I know the hacienda was over 200 years old," describes Munguia. "You had this main house with the four corridors and the fountain in the center. The entrance had huge gates, at least ten or fifteen feet high, wooden doors." A picture comes easily to mind.

"When we would get there it was a big deal. The gates would open and there were all these people, the workers, dressed in white and their huaraches. Generations worked for him. People lived and died within the walls of that compound," describes

Munguia, continuing to add to the scene. "You would see all these little kids running around on this old cobblestone. On one side were the mules, not the donkeys or the horses, the mules. They had to be separated. Then you had the horse barn and then the donkey barn." The rancho produced *pulque*, he notes—a cheap alcoholic beverage once favored by the Aztecs.

However, the setting was merely a prelude to the riding. Munguia's introduction to horses was reminiscent of a scene from *Indiana Jones*, only real. "Uncle Oscar was my hero. We took long rides into a really wild area and to places people have never been, at least not for centuries. We actually rode to one site where we dug out the dirt and found ancient burials." After Munguia's uncle notified the Mexican government, French archeologists came and uncovered an entire town. "This is how I grew up," Munguia remembers, "being in this world of finding arrow tips made out of obsidian from the Indians centuries ago." Horses, however, got left in the wake of adolescence, college, and hotel school in Canada.

Fortune or Fate

Munguia was well along the fast track of Mexico's corporate hotel industry when a new assignment as general manager of the beachside hotel, Plaza Las Glorias, put him on Mexico's Pacific Coast. "I rediscovered horses when I moved to Puerto Vallarta from Cancun. I went on a horseback riding tour, a trail ride, and I loved it!" Munguia recalls. His childhood passion reignited,

Munguia soon sent one of his employees (who conveniently had an equestrian background) to scout prospective mounts for him. He left for Guadalajara the moment a call about equine candidates came in. "I remember walking into this barn and there were ten horses sticking their heads out of stalls, but there was one that I saw and immediately I knew—that was the one." Munguia named the Thoroughbred gelding, an experienced jumper, Heiho. "At the time, I was reading *The Book of the Five Rings*; it's a Japanese samurai book. Heiho is like the path of good."

Back in Puerto Vallarta, Munguia set about learning everything horse-related he could with the same zeal that propelled his hotel career. "I just opened this door to a new world. I loved it. I used to get up at seven in the morning and ride on the beach and then go to work at the hotel." Munguia contacted the owners of vacant land next to the hotel and got permission to build a one-horse barn for Heiho, complete with ceiling fans, automatic water dispenser, and his own private groom (a young woman from France). "I used to take lunch breaks and just spend time with the horse. Sometimes he would be lying down. Eventually, I was able to walk into the barn, talk to him, walk into his stall, and just lie on him, this massive horse, like a big huge dog. I would push his neck and his head and he would lie down totally. That's trust. I developed such a closeness. We had an understanding and I knew it was very special," describes Munguia. "He was my first real horse that I paid for, that I supported. He was very enlightening."

Less than a year after Heiho's purchase, Munguia was in a serious car accident one rainy Puerto Vallarta night, which put him in the hospital for two months, followed by a three-month convalescence at his parents. "Basically, I became a paraplegic, almost a quadriplegic. I was in a wheelchair. It was bad. I had spinal cord injuries," Munguia describes. "But a great part of my rehabilitation took place because one day I decided to get back on a horse, and I got back on that horse." He would mount with help, lifted from the wheelchair by friends, and when he was ready to get off, he would ride beneath a tree branch and hoist himself up. After the horse was led from beneath him, Munguia was carefully lowered into the wheelchair again. "The first encouraging moment to me was when I was able to get on a horse. Once I was on, I didn't need any help, even though I didn't have use of my legs. It was an exciting time for me because I could move; I could walk from point A to point B on the horse."

At the time, Munguia had three doctors—a neurosurgeon, an orthopedic surgeon, and a sports medicine rehabilitation doctor. None of them knew he had gotten back on a horse when he began riding Heiho again. In fact, Munguia had been told he could not ride. Even so, one doctor's words about "real rehabilitation" taking place when life is lived as normally as possible again, got him thinking. "To me it made more sense to be on a horse. When I told them I had ridden, they were like, 'Oh my God!' but then the rehab doctor said, 'Well, wait a minute.'" After lengthy discussions, all three of his doctors subsequently approved the riding. "I felt more comfortable on the horse than in the wheelchair. When I rode at first, I had a body brace and leg braces." In his mind, there's no question of the horse's role in his recuperation. "I don't think it would have been as fast or as strong if I had not been involved with horses," says Munguia. "From then on, I felt 'I can do this' and I kept doing it."

Munguia didn't return to the corporate hotel world; he instead launched his own hotel operation after he was ready to work again. By the late 1980s, he had also built a riding club in Puerto Vallarta and was marketing horseback riding holidays that combined accommodations at Los Tules Resort on the beach with a generous amount of surf, sun, and saddle time. (For a time, the riding holidays were among one airline's frequent flier offerings.) After Mexico's economy took one too many nose-dives, the club was sold and riding holidays ceased in the 1990s. "That was not ever really looked at as a business. The satisfaction to me is just to be involved with horses."

Hoofbeats to Health

"I got used to having the kind of horse that you can identify with. It's like you and him; that's how I felt," says Munguia, recalling a proud, gray Azteca stallion, the most recent of his memorable equine friends. "Sometimes, they say some people live through their memories. I'm not going to do that. I'm just waiting for the right horse and the right situation. Lately, it wasn't favorable for me to have that special horse. I do miss that, but it's going to come." The gracious hotelier adds, "I know that's what I need."

For now, he rides when time and opportunities gel, savoring moments in the saddle. "Most of the riding I've done lately is going to the beach in Puerto Vallarta with my friend, or alone," explains Munguia. "Sometimes you don't even talk the whole way; you ride. Or you talk while you're getting to the beach. Once you're on the beach, it's like that's where you're supposed to be. You can feel the horse's excitement and how they smell the ocean and feel the sand. They look around; everything is so new to them, the boats, the people, the umbrellas. Yet, they feel so free. They're like, 'Wow!' It's such an open space. You give them some rein and they go!"

◯ TRY THIS

Ride by the virtual corral and visit the Inner City Slickers Web site at *www.innercityslickers.org*. Spend some time outdoors with a friend or spouse (horses optional) and each give the Slickers exercise your best shot—what was the worst day and best day you can recall? (For sure, there's something you haven't discussed before.) Take time to make private notes later on about how you felt revealing it. Now for the fun—this is ideally done solo to get the full effect. Do a little field research on the subject of "prejudging." Dress in "costume," go to a restaurant (not a usual hangout), and observe how you are treated. Choose a place where you will be served, even just for coffee, versus a self-service-type setting. If you're a real city slicker, dress like a cowboy or cowgirl. If you're the real McCoy, or another equine professional whose normal garb says "horse," borrow a lab coat, hospital scrubs, or come up with your own version of "theme-type" attire that might indicate a different occupation. How differently are you treated simply because of your attire? How do you feel (besides silly)? By the way, if you encounter someone wearing Western boots, be sure to ask, "Do you ride horses?" Notice what you're thinking before and after you ask. If you're hankering for information on the North American Riding for the Handicapped Association, stop by *www.narha.org*.

Chapter Five

Harmony
. . . a horse chorus

*Horses put people
together, people from all
different fields. They are the
great equalizer . . .*
—João Oliveira

SARAH OLIVEIRA SHIFTS ALMOST IMPERCEPTIBLY IN HER CHAIR, with the slight discomfort of a well-mannered young lady being put on the spot. She's not used to being interviewed by a journalist—especially in English. Even so, her eyes sparkle, the unmistakable shade of Oliveira green shared by her father, home in Belgium, and her uncle João Oliveira, who is sitting across the table with an iced beverage relaxing outside the house. Early this morning before the August temperatures climbed, they drove to Malibu, where she helped him ride nine Lusitano stallions he is educating in the finer nuances of equestrian arts—from start to finish.

João mentions his niece's surprise at finding herself somewhat of a celebrity on her first visit to California, particularly her surprise at some of the responses she's encountered from equestrians hearing her family name. His father, and Sarah's grandfather, was the celebrated Portuguese Classical Master Rider, Nuno Oliveira (who died in 1989), whom many call the link between the great European riders of centuries past and the rise of modern dressage throughout the world. "He was really a fantastic man dedicated to the horse and to his art—before anything else," says João. Revered in his own right, João's known much of the world as his workplace because of the tradition he continues. "Yes, I'm a professional, but for me horses are a way to be in life. Those moments are the moments that count."

The sound of a sliding glass door draws immediate attention as Rebecca Bayot emerges and joins her guests at the table—instantly enlivening the conversation. João's companion of nine years, Rebecca (Becky to friends), is the mother of their seven-year-old son Nuno Oliveira, his grandfather's namesake.

Based now in Los Angeles, they moved from Portugal to the United States in 2002, when João accepted an appointment as Classical Master Rider for Robinson Lusitanos, one of the country's largest (and newest) breeders of a horse long linked to European royalty and steeped in the history of the Iberian Peninsula. It's a world where harmony is often referenced in terms of unity between horse and rider.

Tuned to Horses

Born in Lisbon, João's equestrian education began in earnest at three-and-a-half years old. "I remember following my father everywhere," says João, describing how the two of them would depart at three and four in the morning and cross a river by boat, before heading south of Lisbon to reach his father's horses. João's earliest memory of riding remains ingrained upon his mind. "It ran away with me, but it ran away in cadence. Because I was a little kid and I was moving too much [in the saddle], he started doing all these movements, flying changes every stride." The horse, who had somewhere in the neighborhood of eleven years' training, was apparently doing his best to interpret presumed cues from the small body shifting atop his back. "It was superbly trained," João explains.

Once he reached school age, riding his father's horses became the reward for good grades.

"From them I learned all the [classical riding] movements," remembers João. "The most important thing is to work with the best trained horses to learn to feel those movements in a very natural way." João continues, "I started very early and my father was very hard with me. But I thank him for that. It allowed me to learn." João has recently surpassed a goal he set once: spending fifty years on the back of a horse.

"All my life I've known what is good in terms of classical riding. I was there every day. I learned to recognize what was good because I saw fabulous riders every day." By the time he reached his early teens, João was helping his father train horses and give lessons at the Oliveira School in Avessada, Portugal. He later worked at the school with his father and continued its operation after his death. Yet for all the intensity of his professional career, João discusses horses more like a philosopher. Laughing and smoking with European ease, João makes Portugal seem a sentence away.

The Emotion Quotient

"With certain horses, all the world stops around you. It's like certain women," proclaims João, who has conducted Classical Dressage exhibitions from Asia to Peru to his native European homeland. He has trained horses for clients around the globe, including some that went on to compete internationally at events like the Pan American Games.

Yet the spirit of the horse seems to drive him. "It's a feeling for me, a feeling before everything else. You develop a technique through the years and you must learn that, but it's all about feelings."

Becky, who met João at a clinic he gave, shares a story about riding in a class with him at the Oliveira School, when neither technique nor feeling were on her side. Her first attempt at "passage" (think elevated, springy trot) took place aboard an exquisitely trained stallion named Donizetti, who virtually accomplished the movement on automatic pilot. When João left the class to take a phone call, Becky discovered she couldn't get Donizetti to stop. "It was my first time to do that movement. They forgot all about me and I didn't know how to say, 'Stop!'"

The family members and guests now munching appetizers around the patio table outside are about to be entertained as Becky continues the story. "I'd never been on a horse like that and I was scared to touch the reins. I thought I'd do the wrong thing. The other students said, 'Never ask João; just do what he says.' But what do you do when your teacher goes on the phone and you can't stop the passage! I was giving signals to the other girls in class asking, 'How do you stop?' They're all like, 'Straighten your back.' But I didn't have the right position, so the horse didn't stop."

A near-buckskin color with chocolate-brown legs, Donizetti was the last horse chosen by João's father Nuno, a week before his death. João subsequently trained the horse, a parting gesture to his father and a tribute to his legacy of "the art of riding." João expresses a sentiment that could be a guidepost for the art of living. "You must love what you are doing with the horses. It's more than the technique. The kind of riding that they do in competitions to me is technique, technique, technique. That is not really the school that I was from . . . it was more by our heart."

In turn, the connection goes full circle. "It's a fabulous sensation when I'm on a horse. With certain special horses, you can have a communication where you completely forget your problems and feel good," João reflects.

Becky's brown eyes warm at the thought of one particular horse now in training with João, a dark brown stallion named Nódulo. "It's difficult as a European person in the United States—it's a cultural difference," says Becky. (Herself born in Guam, she has lived in several countries, including Portugal, although mostly the United States.) "But you know, the soothing balm for his soul was Nódulo. João told me, 'This horse understands me the minute I'm on his back.'"

The conversation hops across the table like a bouncing ball as João remembers his father's advice for dealing with troubles, "I remember my father many years ago saying, 'Keep riding your horses and don't worry.'"

In her own experience, Becky owned a succession of three Lusitano stallions (two Oliveira-trained) while in Portugal. A casual rider at most as a girl (riding was more her mother's agenda), Becky established strong relationships with her own horses when she began riding again as an adult. She says that when she thinks of a place where she's ridden, she automatically thinks of the horses she knew there. "A horse can make you feel like you're capable of doing anything, even if you're not a master rider, or even a talented rider. It's kind of like he has wings on his feet and takes you above every little difficulty you have with riding. He lifts up your spirit."

Lofe, a gray Lusitano stallion with a gift for imparting the breed's legendary bravery, came close to emulating the proverbial knight on a white horse, without the knight, for her. "He's the kind of horse that I could ride in the middle of a parade and I'd know he'd take care of me," comments Becky. And he did, amidst throngs of horseback revelers at Portugal's age-old horse fair in Golegã.

Ultimate Equine Ensemble

Each November the town of Golegã, an hour and a half from Lisbon, becomes a Mecca for Lusitanos and the humans they associate with. Drawing thousands of visitors and participants from European royalty to gypsies, the annual horse fair, Feira

Nacional do Cavalo Golegã, teems with riders, reunions, centuries-old traditions, and the wafting scent of freshly roasted chestnuts, as breeders sell and show off their prized stock.

"To go there was a kind of religion. We brought our best horses to show," says João. "Sometimes you don't see friends all year because you are so busy with life—with horses. There, we have time to play, to tell jokes, to drink." (Occasionally, horses are ridden into the bars.)

Her first year attending the horse fair, Becky remembers João creating a minor spectacle aboard Donizetti in a parking lot, amidst a deluge of rain. "All of a sudden, this crowd was building up in the parking lot—you know how small the parking lots in Europe are. My friends and I were wondering what was happening. It was João riding Donizetti in between cars! It was a small circle between ten cars. He was doing pirouettes on the horse! So instead of watching what was going on in the fair, everyone was going to the parking lot to watch João ride the horse in between cars."

João laughs, "You choose your special moment, when you feel, 'Now I'm going to ride and stop the fair.'" More laughter explodes from the dark-haired man as he lights up a cigarette.

Several years later, an impromptu performance was repeated, this time together with Luisa Valença, a noted Portuguese equestrian and long-time Oliveira family friend. The location, however, was not the parking lot, but directly in front of a breeder friend's stand. Again, Golegã's skies dumped a river of its traditional rain. Becky recollects, "Everyone was watching and here comes Luisa Valença and João and they decide to do a number—a little Pas de Deux—just playing around."

João interjects, "For our own pleasure."

Becky explains, "It wasn't to show off this time, it was because they were enjoying it. The horses were enjoying it." Not that this would be her cup of tea, "I mean, how could you enjoy riding with mud up to here, rain pouring, umbrellas everywhere, the crazy fair going on all around, and you're in a small area with a crowd of gypsies passing in front of you? But you could see that Luisa and João were enjoying it." For the occasion, João was riding the bay stallion Infalivel (which Becky later bought). "Women fell in love with that horse and he knew it," remarks Becky. "He has a sex appeal."

Five years after her first trip to Golegã, Becky worked up the nerve to participate in a key ritual of the week-long event. Riding at the fair on St. Martin's Day, November eleventh, is said to ensure good luck for the coming year. But it's not for the faint of heart. On St. Martin's Day, hundreds upon hundreds of horses and riders jam the central arena, circling around a track amidst a wild collection of equine elite to cantankerous ponies.

"I was afraid to ride in that fair," remembers Becky. Five hundred or 600 horses going around and some of them are not from master riders. I was just so nervous." Dressed impeccably in traditional Portuguese costume, with earrings, gloves, and hairstyle exactly as prescribed, the prospect of riding amidst the rowdy pack caused a last minute case of stage fright, even with Luisa Valença (of João's impromptu Pas de Deux) lined up as a riding buddy and for moral support. Normally a teetotaler, Becky downed several glasses of wine to calm her nerves. By the end of two planned rounds on the track, the once-apprehensive rider had managed to get a Scotch in one hand and was suggesting several more loops at the trot or canter. Luisa convinced Becky it was time to stop when six rounds sealed their St. Martin's good luck.

Harmonic Convergence

"The two most marvelous creatures God created were women and horses. You have to ride a lot to see what is good," grins João. "At my age," he laughs, "I need some artificial things to still impress women. If you have the right horse, it is very easy." A harmonious flow of new possibilities can emerge when horses and humans align.

"I've met fabulous people all around the world through horses," explains João. "I think one thing that is common to all those people that came to study with my father and me, is the desire to improve, to do things with better quality and in fact, improve their horses." He adds, "We are all trying to find the ideal horse, but this is a thing that doesn't exist." But put the horse in balance and new possibilities appear, not unlike life itself.

In three weeks, Sarah, João's niece, returns to Belgium. She is headed to Universal Studios tomorrow—one of only a few days not targeted for horses, even on this first trip to Los Angeles.

"I always travel from horse people to horse people. Nearly all the time, it's to see horses." However, this Oliveira plans to study architecture at college soon, attracted to the interconnected duality of creation and organization involved. For now, at João and Becky's, the intent is simply to ride. "I really concentrate, especially here with João. I just want to do everything perfectly. I don't really care about people coming to see me ride. I just want to learn more."

♄ Try This

Find an annual event with horses in your area. Parades are ideal— many include horses, even in small towns. If you're an equestrian, consider riding in the event if you have a suitable mount, or otherwise, participating as a volunteer. Experience the harmony of horse people from many walks of life coming together (and navigating a parade route). Consider Santa Barbara's Old Spanish Days Fiesta, which takes place in August each year. First held in 1924 in this California seaside town, it features one of the country's largest equestrian parades (including horse-drawn floats). For details, see *www.oldspanishdays-fiesta.org* and look for "The Fiesta Historic Parade." Information on Portugal's annual Feira Nacional do Cavalo Golegã can be found at *www.horsefair lusitano.org*.

Chapter Six

Balance
. . . the E in equilibrium

The philosophy of the Tao has a basic respect for the balance of nature, and if you are sensitive you don't upset that balance. Instead you try to find out what it is doing, and you go along with it . . .
—Alan Watts, *What Is Tao?**

HERE IN THE HEART OF KENTUCKY HORSE COUNTRY, THE ELECTRONIC chirp of an alarm clock heralds the dawn of a new day. Cardiologist Mini Das launches from bed and throws on some clothes. The countdown until her 7:00 A.M. shift at Baptist East Hospital in Louisville has begun, and seven horses are waiting for breakfast before she departs.

*Copyright © 2000 by Mark Watts. Reprinted with permission of New World Library, Novato, CA. www.newworldlibrary.com or 800-972-6657 ext 52.

"My whole family, for generations, are doctors: both my parents, my sister, my uncles, my aunts. My dad pushed us all to be physicians. I rebelled against it for awhile," recalls Dr. Das, who was born in Kottayam, India, and moved to England with her parents at age seven. "I didn't know for sure that I was going to enjoy it until I was actually in my third year of medical school, when you start doing the hands-on work. After that, it was easy."

Das was ten when her family relocated to the United States, where her parents' work prompted moves from Indiana to Michigan to Texas, and to Alabama. Horses entered her life via a curious crossroad—the impending prospect of college and a very conservative father. Das agreed to attend Judson College, an all-girls Baptist school close to home on the condition she got to take riding lessons.

Tipping the Scale

"From the moment that I started with them, horses were something I could relate to, something that just felt right. It was grounding for me," says Das. "Up until then, I had to deal with kind of a mixed batch of things in constant conflict—my Indian heritage versus growing up here. You've probably seen all those TV programs about different cultures, and people trying to fit in and getting caught in the middle. That was me for awhile."

After six months of riding lessons, the petite 5'2½" freshman was eager for a horse of her own. "I didn't have much contact with horses until I went to college, then it was just wham," remembers Das. "Horses gave something to me mentally and emotionally. When you touch them, they just give something back. When you're on their backs and you feel them beneath you, there's a security."

Das mentions the fact that some connection with animals is "in her genes," albeit not with horses. Her grandfather worked with elephants for a time as a forest ranger in India and her father even rode one to school while a child in a mountain community.

Yet, convincing her father to buy her a horse required a new measure of independence and ingenuity to literally tip the scales. "I was kind of scrawny. My dad always said I was underweight. He told me I could get the horse if I gained ten pounds," explains Das. "I stuffed myself and stuffed myself. We even found the horse and got him on a trial basis, but I just could not get the weight up." Rather than risk losing the animal she already had set her heart on, the emboldened young woman stuffed her jeans pockets with rocks and made her "successful weight gain" pronouncement in the midst of a gathering of friends and family, where it raised little suspicion. "I hated to do it," Das admits. However, her father conceded, she got the horse, and horses have been a presence in her life since—in steadily increasing numbers. At last count, the equine contingent included show horses, a yearling, and a twenty-two-year-old mare named China, who's been with Das since medical school.

"They all move everywhere I go," says Das, who did her residency at the Mayo Clinic in Rochester, New York. The doctor's successive career advancements have entailed horse relocations from state to state.

"Whenever we moved to a new place, I could tell if it was a good spot or if there was somebody not right if I gauged it by China. She always tells me if there's something wrong. It's really funny, she's a great judge of character," remarks Das, a lithe brunette with a thousand-watt smile.

Before buying a twenty-three-acre farm on the outskirts of Louisville, the doctor contended with boarding her personal herd for years, driving to the barn at the end of twelve-hour shifts at the hospital. At one point while working in Minnesota, Das made two trips to the stable each day—one at four o'clock in the morning to ride before work, in addition to faithful evening rides. By the time Das moved to Kentucky, finding a home where her horses could also live had become a top priority.

"The horses definitely come first," says Das, who went to great lengths to find horse-friendly property near Louisville. Finally settling on acreage with an eighteen-stall barn and an indoor riding arena set amidst rolling fields of Kentucky bluegrass, she promptly christened it Safe Harbor Farm. "We looked at a lot of places," says Das. Recently married, Das met her husband in a chance encounter at a stable where her horses were once boarded.

Less concerned with personal comforts than accommodating their equine companions, the couple opted to convert the barn's kitchen, office, and a former stall into temporary living quarters while a house is built so they could move to the farm with the horses. Das momentarily reflects on the pillar they've come to represent. "They are pretty much involved with every aspect of my life." One particular horse even facilitated her professional path.

Steadying Influence

"I used to get so nervous about tests," says Das, remembering the constant shadow of exams while a medical student. Dealing with the issues of a once abused Thoroughbred proved to be the key for changing that. "China's supersensitive and it used to be hard to ride her when I'd go to the horse show because I had to be calm," remarks Das, who first encountered the mare when she was donated to the college in a fragile state of mind.

It took nine months to get the horse to walk quietly, Das recalls. But the two bonded quickly and soon it was all uphill. "She taught me how to focus, because if I didn't relax, if I was tense, one little twitch and she'd change her lead or she'd get nervous and uptight and you couldn't do anything with her. She taught me that when I first started taking her to the horse shows and it helped me with my test-taking skills in medicine," explains Das, who's ridden competitively in amateur hunter divisions since school. "Because I had to learn how to focus on her, I then began to use that same focus before a test. I'm not brilliant at test taking, but I learned to get through fine. I'm so much more focused than I ever was because of her."

It's been more than a decade since the thirty-six-year-old doctor acquired China, who subsequently became a cherished broodmare. Each of the four offspring occupies a special part of Das's heart, in addition to supplying a home-grown supply of jumping horses. "They'll never be sold. I can't bear to part with them," she explains. The biggest gift China has bestowed on her is a lesson about never giving up on others, Das remarks.

The Equine Ingredient

"I think it's a unique passion and I think it's especially important that people come into contact with horses when they're young or when they're in troubled times," remarks Das. "I've seen so many people gravitate toward horses who had something going on emotionally that horses helped them with. Maybe that's just life in general, but these people are not sitting at home moping. They're out there doing something creative with the horse and I think anything that lets you do that is good for your health."

This is not to say that there aren't things that can be carried to an extreme. Das has witnessed individuals who ignored chest pains to feed their horses first, and then land in the emergency room with full-blown heart attacks. Hence the case for balance.

"In my mind, emotionally, there is no doubt that horses have helped me. I love challenges. I think that is partly why I love working, but with horses, it's also something very spiritual," Das reflects. "You feel something in yourself when they do well. It's like you've triumphed. It gives you back a sense of peace and security. It's almost like they're not the ones that are winning, it's you," she adds.

After twelve hours of nonstop activity at the hospital, the sacred hour arrives again. Das makes a beeline home to the welcome of whinnies. "I have four that are ridable right now, so I rotate who gets done according to what their issues are." Beneath lights illuminating her indoor riding arena, the cardiologist climbs aboard two or three horses before calling it a night. "I have so much stress at work. When I get to the barn, I brush them, clean out their feet, and ride. Everything else is out of my mind. I don't have to think about a patient, somebody not doing well, or doing anything else." Across the country in Beverly Hills, someone Das has never met would understand exactly what she's talking about.

A Moment of Stillness

"Hold all calls," says Catherine Olim, managing director at the Hollywood public relations powerhouse PMK/HBH, on the other end of the telephone. For a few moments, the incessant rounds of media calls and celebrity clients stand still as she relaxes in her chair and talks horses.

"Like most little girls, I just adored horses," remarks Olim, who began riding at seven years old near her childhood home outside Memphis. Her teacher was the mother of 1984 Olympic equestrian team gold medalist, Melanie Smith Taylor, notes Olim. As usual, the horse world has suddenly shrunk the globe.

"It's funny, so many of my clients, actors, have daughters who are becoming terrific riders. They take it quite seriously and the parents are very supportive," the PR maven remarks. As for her own involvement, Olim found the recreational side of horses won out when her interests rekindled as an adult.

"I have so much pressure, competition, and stress in my work-a-day life that I need the opposite in what I do for pleasure," explains Olim, who lived in New York City for a number of years before moving to California. "Trail riding really affords me that. It is a complete escape. You're out in nature and it's you and the horse and some friends. It's a great way to get together with people. The phone's not ringing. I've had terrific conversations on trail rides."

Unless she's out of town on press junkets, at film festivals, or touring with celebrity clients, most weekends find Olim on a horse in Malibu, not far from the ocean breezes of Zuma Beach. The day's agenda often includes riding in the Santa Monica Mountains, just minutes inland from the coast. "There are occasionally hairy moments; because horses can be unpredictable, things happen. But generally speaking, I find it enormously relaxing," says Olim. "There are miles of trails and sometimes you see no one. Different years you have different wildflowers growing. The flora changes all the time." An avid gardener, Olim further notes, "That's one of the things I like about riding tours." In fact, the lure of riding in Ireland was what stoked the coals of her childhood horse interest.

Symmetry in the Saddle

"I rode a little in college and just a little when I moved to New York City. You don't really ride in the city," remembers Olim. But the day the *New York Times* ran an article about riding at Castle Leslie in Ireland, the publicist shook the dust off her boots. "I started going regularly to Northwest Connecticut to a friend's house. We started really goosing up the amount of riding we were doing." Olim enjoyed the area and being back in the saddle so much, she began renting a house there on weekends. After a flurry of cross-country riding lessons, the friends packed their bags for Ireland.

"I was not as comfortable with riding at that point because I hadn't been doing it enough. I was pretty tense, but got through the trip anyway and enjoyed it," describes Olim. It also spawned an immediate interest in European riding holidays. "For me, it's a great way to take a vacation. You're with people, but you can go back to your room at night and have a little solitude. It's an extraordinary way to see the countryside. You don't have windows to roll down and engines in the way. I just adore it."

In contrast to the sightseeing of tour buses and itinerary-filled groups, Olim's seen Tuscany and Provence, among other destinations, from the back of a horse. "I have a very fond memory of a ride in Spain that was quite arduous and a little scary at times. I'm terrified of heights and sometimes we were on very narrow trails on a precipitous hillside for hours." However, breathtaking foliage and an intimate encounter with nature more than compensated for the route. "Sometimes we would be walking across meadows and it was like horseback aromatherapy," Olin recalls.

The E in Equilibrium

For someone who's never tried it, one might assume that anyone who's ridden regularly for eighteen years would certainly own her own horse. However, the "E" (correct answer: "equine") in equilibrium, does not necessarily mean ownership. "I really stressed out for the brief amount of time I owned a horse," admits Olim, who purchased a hunter-jumper after moving to Los Angeles. "Horses can be enormously expensive creatures to maintain. It's always amazed me that something that can be that strong can also be so fragile. Any time you have an animal that you fall in love with, there's a big emotional commitment and a financial commitment."

The truth about balance and horses is that you don't need to own one to find it. Millions of equestrians experience it via leasing, lessons, camps, and an infinite array of four-legged routes.

Until Olim's next horseback holiday abroad, the weekend rides in Malibu will work magic for the woman whose celebrity-driven profession requires a constant balancing act. The moments spent in the saddle travel with her wherever she goes.

"It sort of encompasses everything in life—fear, joy, relaxation, stress, a little bit of everything. It's a challenge because horses are very individual. They're not a bicycle. A horse has its own mind and its own emotional makeup, so you have to work with him," reflects Olim. "Horses are really good barometers for how you're feeling. If you're nervous, they know it and it makes them nervous. If you're not in charge, they're in charge. I think for the most part, they're very honest creatures—straightforward creatures," which is something anyone in Hollywood can appreciate.

☊ TRY THIS

Ready to rebalance mind-body-soul with a stint in the saddle? Spend a long weekend at a guest ranch. Particularly in the Southwest and California, many are close enough to major airports that four-day, three-night stays are not only feasible in terms of travel time, they also include special packages targeting different riding levels. For instance, the Alisal Guest Ranch and Resort, forty minutes north of Santa Barbara in Solvang, California, has beefed up special offerings for new riders with annual Cowgirl Boot Camps. Opened in the 1950s, the Alisal marries traditions like no phones or TVs in the rooms, with the "casual elegance" of a French chef and assorted amenities. Other ranches feature clinics with top horse industry names along with your stay. That said, the next word is "Whoa"! If your normal life is filled with schedules and nonstop activity, leave the special packages until next time. Instead, find a ranch with plentiful leisurely riding opportunities. Some are more schedule-driven than others. Ask about the availability (and price) of private or semiprivate rides with a guide and picnic lunch.

Two excellent sources for guest ranch information and locations include the Dude Ranch Ranchers' Association at *www.dude ranch.org* and Gene Kilgore's Online Guide to Ranch Vacations at *www.ranchweb.com*. Before you go to a ranch, buy a cheap spiral notebook. Take a black marker and write "Horsing Around" on the cover and draw a stick horse underneath. (Time limit: two minutes!) On the first page inside, list five things you are feeling about the trip before you depart. (You have thirty seconds—no cheating!) Each day you spend at the ranch, list five idiosyncrasies of the horse you rode and five things that stood out about the environment (sights, smells, sounds). Write down any dreams the following morning. At the end of your visit, describe in one word how it feels to see your luggage packed and ready to leave. One week after your return home, read everything you wrote and look for the single sentence or word that stands out. Highlight it. Consider the fact that you actually took a vision quest—the word that stood out is a gift from the horse path to you.

Lastly, but not least, for those already immersed in horses: your assignment involves one sheet of notebook paper. This is short, since that's probably how much time is left in your evening after a day with horses. Fold the paper in half lengthwise and number one through five on each side. On the left side, list five attributes of your favorite horse. On the right side, list five things you might do if you weren't involved with horses. Look at the paper in one month. Is your favorite horse showing you something that needs more balance in your life? In other words, don't ignore chest pains to feed the horse.

Chapter Seven

Communication
... the whinnying combination

*Horses can perceive your
feelings, they can perceive some of
your attitudes. They can certainly
perceive your moods ...*

—Reaves F. Nahwooks

"I GREW UP WITH HORSES. I'M A MEMBER OF THE COMANCHE TRIBE," says Reaves Nahwooks.

"When I was just a kid, my grandfather gave me a horse, a Paint, that was given to him from one of the big ranches in Texas. In those days, ranchers used to come through here, and of course, they honored many of the Native American people with live-stock—giving them livestock," he clarifies.

"Horses were one of the most important parts of our culture. The Comanches take pride in calling themselves 'Horsemen of the Plains.'"

71

Born near Oklahoma City, Nahwooks worked for many years at Fort Hall, Idaho, in a community development capacity. In 1986, he retired after thirty-four years of service with the federal government and then enrolled in seminary school with his wife. At the time, he was also raising and racing both Thoroughbreds and Appaloosas.

"I don't think there's any question in my mind that horses are significant in our culture, but they're also significant in one's life," comments Nawhooks, now the pastor at Rainy Mountain Kiowa Indian Baptist Church in Indiahoma, Oklahoma—a small town twenty miles west of Lawton in the southwest portion of the state. "My perspective is that animals, or anything that God made— however you perceive God—is spiritual and even planned."

Speaking Through Silence

Nahwooks contemplates, "Communication many times is through silence. I'm convinced that one can communicate with animals, especially horses. You can sit and look at a horse and if you're very intense about it, you will be able to communicate. If you're around them enough, you will know if there's something wrong. You'll know when they're full of life, or there's happiness, whatever there is in a horse."

For a moment, Nahwooks pauses, carefully choosing the words to explain a way of knowing that comes without step-by-step instructions. "Just by being quiet and silent, you can tell whether they're hungry, or they want a drink, or something else. You can't read their minds, but certainly you can know what kinds of options they might like. Of course, you can tell when a horse is sick. These elements don't come from talking, although I think you can (verbally) talk to them, too," says Nahwooks, continuing the thought, "I believe they understand."

Like meditation, communicating through silence begins with quieting the mind. When the roar of mental chatter and thinking quell, perception of a horse, one's surroundings, or even self, can become infinitely clearer.

"Tribal people have almost a diametrically opposite mode and behavior than Western society. I could give you a long list of differences, for example, how do you define power? You look in the dictionary and you've got twenty-five definitions. Basically, it is the ability to make something happen. But the definition of power that Native American people have is not in the dictionary. We perceive power to be healing medicine and supernatural," explains Nahwooks. "And it is that way with Spirit. Spirit is also how we tie in with God."

The minister elaborates, sending threads of the concept in rapid motion. "A place that is sacred basically is where you've had a spiritual experience. That's why many times you associate a lot of that with a vision quest—it's a revelation or a message that's supposed to give you guidance. I think our perceptions of animals enter into that. At times, animals will talk to you. If you're an outdoors person, you can sit and be quiet and hear all the noises around you—early in the morning or late in the evening are both good times. You can become acquainted with sounds of birds or animals, whatever it is around." Nahwooks comments, "I'm convinced that horses have a personality—without a question."

Talking Traditions

Little of the Comanche culture and history was documented in writing before 1900, notes Nahwooks, "at least by Indian people." Instead, what was mostly recorded were "basically impressions written by Army officers, missionaries, and educators." He explains, "That doesn't mean we don't have the history. We retained it by passing it on from generation to generation, through oral history. Of course, many of our stories centered around horses."

Nahwooks gives a brief history lesson—how the Comanches once claimed all of Texas and why they moved to Oklahoma. He describes, "Oklahoma was far enough away to be out of reach of the Mexican Army, but it was still close enough the Comanches could ride to Mexico on horses for revenge if they needed to. There was a lot of that."

Horses played a prominent role in many aspects of the culture. "Warriors had some of the best-trained horses. They knew what to do in certain situations. They were trained to hunt. They were also trained for war." Nahwooks makes another point—Comanches excelled in breeding. "They bred them to be the best runners, the strongest for war, and they had them for fun and games. They had racehorses for contests and trained them for that also."

One fallacy Nahwooks attributes to society's romance with Western movie images is the association of Native Americans with Paint horses. "Comanches predominately preferred buckskin horses with black manes," he notes. "Also coveted were gray horses with black manes, or a white horse." Not that the colorful Paint breed was totally excluded. "They liked them, too," Nahwooks notes. "In fact, I had a whole herd of them when I was growing up because my grandfather had given me a Paint horse." The mare, named Nellie, lived almost forty years.

More Than a Feeling

"I grew up on that horse. I rode bareback most of the time," remembers Nahwooks. "Just like you drive cars, we rode those horses every place we went, whether for recreation, to visit with people, whatever." But their mounts weren't just vehicles; they were teammates in games. One called "pull off, push off" could be likened to "tag" on horses.

Nahwooks recalls the contest, "We were pretty rough and reckless. We'd ride alongside each other and pull each other off the horses. Of course, you learn to ride that way—you learn to take care of yourself. In other words, part of our physical growth centered around the horses. We all had horses, more than one—our parents did too, and our grandparents."

Spirit takes on a different connotation in this context, Nahwooks notes. "I think a coordination or a cooperation—you have to be of similar experience. The spirit of togetherness, of co-ordination, being together—the horse learning what you need and want." In that sense, riding becomes an endeavor of joined intent. Nahwooks thinks out loud, "Horses have moods, just like people. When you love a horse, they know it."

Likewise, the Paint mare Nahwooks owned for nearly four decades conveyed an unequivocal message before departing. "When Nellie got ready to die, she would come around and look at you and stay by the house and do unusual things that you would never expect," he remembers. For the moment, the pastor is uncharacteristically horseless. Yet one gets the clear impression the connection continues nevertheless.

Tuning In

Howard Lee was described by the late author Carlos Casteneda as a teacher and guide whose extraordinary dominion over the nuances of energy merited admiration and respect. After nearly thirty years of private practice, the once reclusive "healer's healer" ceased being a secret. In 1992, Lee founded The Light of Life Institute in Santa Monica, California and began teaching workshops worldwide on his Light of Life energy system to diverse individuals—from real estate magnates, CEOs, and natural health practitioners, to dancers, actors, and equestrians.

"There are some individuals who are born with an affinity for communication with animals. It doesn't mean that they don't have any emotional or mental chatter going on—they just have the ability to broadcast their messages or receive them more clearly than the next person. That particular aspect of their awareness is more enhanced. In a way, it's more abstract, transmitting images and impressions rather than words," explains Lee, who was born in 1939 in China and has dedicated his life to the development and understanding of energetics. "You retrieve a degree of that native ability when you're dealing with foreigners. You don't speak the same language and yet often, you can get quite a bit across. Of course, people will attribute it to gesticulations, but there's more to it than that," he affirms.

"Increasingly, we're finding out that different creatures in the animal kingdom have very sophisticated ways of dealing with reality, but on the surface, it seems very crude and simplistic. I think that there are different vibrations, probably emotions transmitted in sound that's encoded, which we're not privy to." In a way, this parallels media transmissions encoded with digital information, Lee suggests. "Before it is deciphered, a human being cannot make sense of it. It doesn't even register if there's electronic or photonic encoding. Nonetheless, it's there."

A man whose trim, youthful appearance belies his years, Lee returns the conversation to the four-legged domain. "I've said often in a joking manner—but it's absolutely true—when an animal finds a source of food or a water hole, it doesn't go back and tell the other members of its group like we human beings do, 'When you see the tree you turn left, and after you see a rock you turn right, and then you're there.' They just send a picture of how they got to it and the others see the image."

While neither a horse owner nor rider, Lee cites a personal experience illustrating the point. He encouraged a young horse to leave its companions and cross a mucky field for carrots under rather unusual circumstances. "Because it was rainy and muddy, the horses were just standing under the shedrow and didn't want to move. Even though we were waving carrots around, they were just looking, not interested," recalls Lee. "So I just projected. I pictured the horse traipsing across some grassy spots (that weren't muddy) and in a few minutes it did just that."

Lee contemplates, "We think that we know everything. The thing is, the meanings of this world are based on limitations. All of your grandest music and most pleasing sights are based within that limit. Anything outside that, you don't even apprehend. If you were able to hear or see a bigger range, it would totally change your world and your reality. In terms of awareness, our visual and auditory abilities are based on narrow parameters of energy. We now know that other animals have much more sophisticated abilities, whether it be hearing or seeing, or even more subtle—able to detect magnetic forces in navigating the earth."

Trained in traditional Chinese medicine and martial arts early in his career, Lee mastered the Choy Lai Fut system of Kung Fu with the late Professor Low Ben, foremost Kung Fu master in the United States. He studied the art of acupuncture with one of America's pioneer acupuncturists, Dr. Gim Shek Ju.

Lee describes the Light of Life energy, which he founded through a process of remembering, as a pragmatic resource that promotes healing and self-transformation, with benefits that include expanded perception and intuitive awareness, sharpened clarity, and creativity, among others.

"Animals, like children, are able to spot someone who is not honest. They can feel your emotions. When a person is afraid, the body emits certain body odors that are associated with fear. Before the body starts to emit such odors, there's already an energetic factor that animals can sense," remarks Lee. "Everything is preceded by an energetic component."

The discussion continues in a vein seldom addressed in his workshops. "While animals don't have the kind of intelligence that we have, they have awareness in a different way. I think they're able to communicate with their owner on a deeper level. Even though the human being doesn't know exactly what it is, they intuitively feel certain comforting, or distress signals, from their charge. It's just like newborn babies communicating with their mothers," explains Lee.

"To some extent, we can cultivate our intuition and our telepathic abilities and be able to communicate with animals on a deeper level. That is absolutely possible."

Featured on national television shows and invited to think tanks during recent trips to Italy and Spain, Lee contemplates, "I've always said that this is a cumulative and incremental reality. Our intellectual attempts to explain the nature of the universe is but a narrow construct of our rational mind. Yes, this has enabled us humans to incrementally build a unique civilization within the greater reality. But our dependence on the rational approach and the use of language has narrowed our focus and obscured our telepathic and psychic abilities."

Lee glances at his watch. It's time to return to the office for a last round of clients before his next workshop tour to Europe or South America. "One of the most powerful things people can do for themselves is to be able to quiet down the mental chatter. When you quiet down, then you begin to access the inner wisdom that's always speaking to you, but you tend to ignore," advises Lee. "It also enables you to have more clarity in seeing the truth of whatever situation applies to you at any given moment."

The Four-Legged Frequency

Chilean horseman and breeder, Jorge Ludwig, winds up one last round of shoulder-height fences aboard a big, bay athletic mare recently flown in from the family farm fourteen air hours away in South America, before dashing out for lunch. His training barn, Ludwig Stable, at Hidden Valley Equestrian Center, is just west of the Ventura County line near Westlake, California. The barn sits on land once owned by Roy Rogers at the end of a tree-flanked road lined with equestrian properties—some advertised in the $50 million range.

"I can see a total turnaround on the horses of fifteen or twenty years ago and today in the way they behave and how they react toward the human being. I'm still not firm on it. So, it's just a theory I have," remarks Ludwig. "Every day you learn something different with horses and this is something that has been growing on my mind. I think the horse is starting to have glimpses of IQ that I did not see years ago. Maybe it's the evolution in the world. You know how people have gotten smarter; I think the horse has, too. The seclusion of the animals with the human is transmitting a lot of things. They're getting smarter." Ludwig's face breaks into a smile as he speculates only partly in jest, "People got into computers and horses got into trailers."

Raised in a family of horse breeders, Ludwig grew up with three brothers at Fundo Pedernal (Pedernal Farm, which his parents still own), 600 miles south of Santiago, during a time of political turmoil in Chile. On one occasion, he and one brother jumped their horses over locked gates at a neighboring farm to escape an uprising they inadvertently encountered. Despite the national chaos, Ludwig attended the elite Bernardo O'Higgins Military Academy in Santiago (a West Point–caliber institution) for most of high school, beating out eighty-four other students to land the only open spot on the show jumping team. In college, after four years of veterinary school, Ludwig abruptly switched to a major in agriculture, just to complete a degree. "The political situation wasn't pretty. The horses kept me sane," he recalls. His degree, however, opened the door to an international agricultural exchange program that brought him to California.

"If you are into horses, you can pretty much go anywhere in the world and makes friends in a hurry," notes Ludwig. His parents took in several contingents of European royalty (horse families) escaping World War II Germany, before his birth. "Horses bring people together," explains Ludwig, who met his wife in California when she approached him for help in purchasing a jumping prospect. By the time a horse was found, the romance was sealed and Ludwig was permanently implanted in North America.

Feeling It Out

"You sense different things when you ride; you become different," reflects Ludwig, now a father of two. "I think it's mainly feeling—physical and emotional. You might drive differently just because you have a better feel from touching the reins and accelerating with your leg on a horse. The horse brings out a lot of senses, which I don't think any other sport will do as clearly. You're dealing with a feeling through your fingertips, your seat, your hands, and your emotions."

Ludwig pauses a moment to emphasize a key communications point. "You cannot lose your cool with a horse. The minute you do, you pretty much lose out. It's better for you to get off and go do something else and start over the next day, or an hour later." He could be discussing the skills required to resolve conflicts with humans.

The trilingual trainer returns his attention to the subject at hand. "Horses teach you a lot—instead of a person talking back to you, they'll act back to you. That's why I think people mentally get a lot out of them. They learn that horses will respond to the way you treat them and they'll do it by acting back." Ludwig continues, "I think body language with the horse is the most important part of the relationship—the way you present yourself to the horse and the approach you have toward it, even when you're on top of him. It's not a verbal language. A lot of people have learned over the years how to have body language. Some people say, 'Talk to your horse.' I think that body language is the talk to the horse."

Ludwig wonders out loud, "Why would you meet some-body and not shake hands? In other countries, people hug and kiss. Even if they don't know someone, they always shake hands. I think it's a good way to get to see who you're dealing with—what kind of a vibration you have toward the other human. That's the way the horse communicates with you when you get on him. It's like shaking hands when you're touching the reins."

On the Same Wavelength

The training barn Ludwig operates in Hidden Valley includes numerous equine relatives, as does his family's farm in Chile. "When I was a kid I always wanted to have a horse that would think just the same way that I thought and we would be best friends," he recalls. "I've known horses that go back eight genera-tions. It's unbelievable, the character never changes if it's domi-nant." Ludwig can identify the great-great-grandmothers of such horses solely on behavior traits.

Alberta, the big mare from Chile, is done with her work for today. By the time Ludwig's checked for phone messages, she will be untacked and getting a bath, courtesy of Ludwig's groom, Alberto. No one would guess that the relaxed horse arrived from another continent just a matter of days before.

Ludwig now in his forties, says the horses he rides refuse jumps less frequently than they did when he was young and more athletic. "Very seldom do I have a horse refusing anymore, even a young horse at the first jump in his life. If you teach a young horse to be relaxed with your body language, they get that right away and go through fire for you," adds Ludwig.

Sometimes the competitive show ring dramatizes the point perfectly. "It is seldom that you just put together a ride so perfect that the horse never has to do just a little bit more than normal to win the class," explains Ludwig. "My daughter, for example, went blistering fast on a course at a show recently. She missed the distance, the horse bailed her out, and she won the class. I don't go and congratulate the daughter. In those cases, most the time I've gone and given the horse a kiss." Finally ready to depart for lunch, Ludwig turns to add a final thought. "It happens almost all the time when you win a big class. You know they did way more than you asked them to do, just to help you out."

◠ TRY THIS

Cultivate your communication abilities. Go out in nature early in the morning or late in the evening and listen to the sounds around you. Pick a number: three, five, or seven. That's the number of days you will spend time in nature at sunrise or sunset—your choice. An apartment balcony can work. If you have a horse setting available, lucky you! Begin the exercise with a conscious moment of gratitude for this special gift. Outdoors, position yourself comfortably and plan to spend at least fifteen minutes in silent observation. Begin with your eyes closed and concentrate on the sounds surrounding you. Listen for birds, insects, and whatever animal sounds you can identify. Halfway through your session, open your eyes and focus on a single spot. Concentrate on colors, distinctive markings, and impressions of any animals present. Otherwise, leaves, sticks, flowers, or the first item you focus on, will suffice. Any notes you care to make will offer later insights. Consider that this is an incremental reality and subsequent days will build on the first.

If you're game for more, find a partner and try this two-person exercise. Sit facing each other about four feet apart. Be sure you can easily make direct eye contact. For five minutes, observe one another silently. Truly look into the other person's eyes and observe impressions that cross your mind. Beginners may find an explosion of laughter or persistent giggles irresistible. Intent, practice, and a true desire to really see another living being will help you focus. At the end of the exercise, share your impressions with each other. You may be surprised to learn that you perceived something clearly that you were never before aware of. Now take your focus to an equestrian setting.

Riding can become a direct route to inner stillness. See how true it is for you. This exercise is particularly geared toward active equestrians with sufficient knowledge and ability. Plan to ride as an exercise in silent communication. Spend time grooming and tacking the horse without talking. Leave your watch behind. While riding, devote your complete attention to the horse and your surroundings. Wind things up when it "feels right." When you dismount, simply observe your inner state. Later, reflect on what insights the process revealed.

Lastly, if the spirit moves you, canter on by the Light of Life Institute at *www.thelightoflife.com* or Ludwig Stable at *www.ludwigstable.com*.

Learn more about the Comanche Language and Cultural Preservation Committee at *www.comanchelanguage.org*.

Chapter Eight

Honesty
. . . the trail of truth

*If you do not hide from yourself, you
do not hide from others either . . .*
—Thomas Cleary

IN A WORLD MEASURED BY YARDS,
not miles, an explosion of Quarter
Horses breaks from the starting gate at Los
Alamitos Race Course just before dusk, bathed in the glow of
spotlights. A gull's jaunt from the saltwater cosmos where the
Queen Mary docks to the west, the track is an easy flight above
the streets of Long Beach as the bird wings homeward before
the last glow of sun drops from sight. Meanwhile, a carload of
spectators pulls into the track, fresh from traffic on the 405
freeway. A veteran parking lot attendant pokes his head in the
window, welcoming everyone by name. Instantaneously, an
unmistakable "down home" feeling melts the multimillion mass

of humanity on both sides of the nearby Los Angeles–Orange County border as the metal turnstiles rotate with each arrival entering the grandstand.

From a side hallway, World Champion race trainer Donna McArthur appears in the lobby wearing crisp denim jeans, a cotton shirt, and Western boots, with delicate diamond cross earrings accented by the cut of her hair. Her pale blue eyes smile a welcome as she quickly escorts a visitor to the stable area. Several horses are being readied for the track, as a Boston terrier inside McArthur's office catches sight of the petite woman and excitedly jumps up and down.

Straight from the Heart

"A horse to me is like dogs are to some people. A dog's always happy to see you. It doesn't matter how bad a day you've had. That's how I've always treated my horses. They can hardly wait to see you if you treat them right," remarks McArthur, whose training barn at Los Alamitos includes fifty strapping Quarter Horses.

Early on, her husband James McArthur—a racehorse trainer whose career was well-established before hers began—shared a truism that she took to heart: "It's just common sense. Like any of us, the talent may be there, but you have to develop it. You have to train them."

The softspoken woman notes, "The thing you have to do is make them like it and not go so far that you stress them out, or get them sore or bored. You have to make it so they like what they're doing, but not go so far that they start rebelling." Her philosophy on training draws repeated parallels between horse and human. "If you would treat a horse like you would treat your child, you would be amazed. Basically it's the same. Some of them are smarter than others, some are super intelligent. Some of them are lazy and you just have to keep working to get the most out of them. Some of them are hyper; some have good days, some don't. Some of them are going to give you all they can every single time. Others have tons and tons of talent and it doesn't matter what you do—they're just uninterested."

McArthur became the first female to win the American Quarter Horse Association's (AQHA) lauded Champion of Champions race and to train a World Champion in 1996, when a three-year-old filly named Dashing Folly won every one of twelve races entered. One year later, McArthur captured the AQHA Champion Trainer award, breaking a stranglehold on the title held by Quarter Horse racing's legendary trainer Blane Schvaneveldt. Victories in the All American Futurity with a horse named Corona Cash and in the Los Alamitos Million with This Snow Is Royal sealed her reputation as a trainer. Come 1999, McArthur set another record as the first trainer to win the Los Alamitos Million Futurity more than once, as Corona Kool streaked across the finish line.

"As far as me ever thinking that I would ever become a trainer or have the success to have the best horses in training that money can buy, I'm amazed," says McArthur, whose speaking voice is reminiscent of Reba McEntire's. In fact, were it not for horses, McArthur's career might have taken a different route.

"I love music. I admire anybody that's got the talent to get up on a stage and sing. I think that's just a gift that God gave some people. If I hadn't been involved with the sport of horses, I might have been a singer." Horses, however have always represented an unequivocal way of life.

On to Truth or Consequences

Born in El Paso, Texas, McArthur moved to a small New Mexico town in fourth grade (where her parents still live), thirty-three miles from the city of Truth or Consequences. Known for its natural hot springs, the city's moniker was adopted from the radio program, once broadcast there. "When we grew up, we had two horses that basically made our living," McArthur recalls. "Sometimes on Saturdays, we would go to horse shows and compete in events. You paid entry fees, but you won money. You didn't just go to ride and not get anything. It was too expensive to haul them. On Sundays, we would go to a rodeo or a roping event and compete there. We did everything on those horses—everything—horse shows, rodeos, you name it. Those horses provided a living for my mom and dad and my three brothers and myself."

Nevertheless, McArthur's early association with horses was not only as an income source. "I remember one mare. She was great. All the neighbor kids would come over and she would come up to the fence and we would all get on and just ride her in the pen with no bridle, nothing. I would ride in the front and they would get up behind." By the time secondary school required

daily roundtrip commutes of sixty-six miles to Truth or Consequences, horses brought an added respite. "We had to ride the
bus so I didn't participate in any of the school events," recalls
McArthur. "Almost every afternoon when I'd get home, I would
ride. If you didn't feel good or you'd had a bad day or whatever,
just to go out there and catch the horse and ride, you could lose
all your frustrations."

The Perfect Pace

McArthur began her own career as a racehorse trainer several
years after marrying James in 1975. (She started as a groom
and worked her way up, receiving her first trainer's license in
1982.) Not surprisingly, the union came through the inter-
secting paths of two horse families. It also came through a con-
fluence of left-handedness. Had her father and James's brother
not shared the trait, her father would not have trained a roping
horse for her future brother-in-law, and she and James might
never have met.

McArthur left the racehorse training to her husband after
their daughter was born. "I was basically a housewife and mother.
I quit for awhile and got refreshed," she explains. She plunged
back into the sport close to two decades later. "I was not real
young then and it was really hard on me," she recalls. "So in
1996, I came [to California] and I learned to pace myself and
had a really good year. I thought, 'This is nice. You can stay here
year-round and not have to move back and forth. That's why I
chose to just stay and race in one place all the time.'" McArthur's

record and ensuing awards quickly confirmed the wisdom of her decision.

Integrity Junction

"You can pretty much make out of it what you want. You don't have to punch a time clock. Nobody's looking over your shoulder if you leave early, or if you come late. You set the pattern of how things have to be done," explains McArthur about life as a race-horse trainer. "You've got to have some self-discipline, some self-respect, and some determination to be successful at it. It's a sport and it's a business."

For her that means arriving by 7:00 A.M. at the track, working until noon, and then heading home for lunch and a quick nap. Around three in the afternoon, McArthur is back to prepare for an evening of racing. Barring unusual circumstances, Mondays are her sole day off.

"If everyday, you take really good care of yourself—and you know how far you can push yourself—you can stay at the top level all the time and compete at your best. The horses are the same," insists McArthur. "If you get just beat down and tired and nobody wants to cooperate, you're just like, 'Ah, forget it.'" It's clearly the same for McArthur as it is for her horses.

McArthur checks her watch and briefly departs to check on a filly making her second start in the next race. Before the horses break from the starting gate, the trainer has taken a seat in the grandstand to visit with clients in town from Washington. The 220-yard race that quickly unfolds is like watching equine sprinters. McArthur is clearly satisfied even though the filly doesn't win. "She did everything pretty much right. She just kind of got a little lost in the middle of the race because the horses were going faster than she was. They knew what to do and she didn't," explains McArthur.

"It's like kids when you send them to school. The first few days they're not real sure if they want to do it or not. If they have a teacher that they like who makes it fun for them, they can hardly wait to go the next day. Same with horses. You've got to give them something that they like. Then, as they learn what to do and they like it more, they're like, 'Man this is fun!'"

One gets the distinct impression that if horse votes counted, McArthur would be named "teacher of the year," especially by the ones arriving with a few miles beneath their feet. "Sometimes you'll get horses from other people and they go to the back of the stall and they just stand there. They're stressed or they're sad or they're just not happy. They're not people-friendly," remarks McArthur. "But most of them will get to where they love people. Mine are all pets. Most of them, you can walk up to the stall and if they're in the back and you talk to them, they'll come up to the front."

One of the toughest parts of the business can be dealing with the human component, the trainer admits. "Some of the people are not very appreciative of their horses. It's like a tool, something to make money for them. The hardest thing to deal with are people who want them to give you their best every time, which they can't always do. Then they're like, 'We'll just throw it away and get a new one.'"

McArthur grows pensive, "Some people want to have a two-year-old that runs for the big bucks and some people want to just have a horse to come watch and have fun. I've got a couple that I just started training for and they just like the sport. If they win it would be fantastic, but that's not the ultimate goal. It's to come and see their horse run in competition. That means a lot to them."

Clearly, it also means a lot to the trainer. "Every time I come to the track, even when I don't have horses racing, I always pray that all the horses and all the riders are safe," mentions McArthur. She points out that racing is the only sport where an ambulance follows the athletes around; those who have seen jockey spills understand why.

"What makes racing fun are the people who love the horse, no matter what it does. Most of them are like, 'Well, it didn't get out of the gate, it didn't do this—all the stuff it didn't do.' But what about all the good stuff that it did do?" asks McArthur, ever the horses' advocate. "There's so much competition and so much money involved. Some people are good losers and some people aren't. And, some can just walk away from a race and say, 'You know, it wasn't my day.'"

Clear and Candid

For all her racing accomplishments and awards, McArthur conveys a humble matter-of-factness about her talents. "I can't make them run any faster than they can run, but if you can train them and get the most out of them—the best out of them—I think I can do that really good," she remarks. "There are some that are fast that have no problems. Some that are fast have a lot of problems and you have to just take care of them; they'll generally let you know when they've had enough. 'We'd better not push him any harder or any farther—that sort of thing.'"

It boils down to an ability to read the horse. "Most of the time, they let you know they're going to do something before they do it, if you can just pick up on it. I think it's something you're born with," reflects McArthur. "If you've been around them long enough, you know if they're going to blow up before they do it. You can see it in their expressions and in their gaits." Such insights apply equally to the trail as to the track. "If you treat horses right, they're going to give back to you double. It doesn't matter if it's competition or if it's just to have them as a friend," she adds.

The scent of an expensive cigar drifts through the air as the bugle calls the next parade of prancing horses to the starting gate. "I do think that everybody has a turn to have good luck, bad luck, whatever," says McArthur. "I think that if you live right and do right and treat people right and are honest with yourself, that sooner or later your number will probably come up and you'll be where you want to be."

The Truth of Excellence

Albert Stern picks up a limited-edition bronze horse sculpture displayed in the cavernous two-story music room at his home in Malibu, California, and smiles. The trophy won by his horse Determined Dash in one leg of Quarter Horse racing's MBNA

Challenge, shares space in the oceanview expanse regularly filled with the unmistakable sound of his 1697 Stradivarius violin.

"There's something very ethereal and almost supernatural when you achieve certain elements of perfection and performance. In music, it goes beyond just playing the right notes at the right tempo, in proper intonation, and in tune. There is something else," reflects Stern, one of the world's most revered violinists. "I guess it's a sense of beauty, a sense of balance, and a sense of rhythm. These are all things that music and these animals have in common." A Quarter Horse breeder for close to three decades, Stern and his wife got involved in racing in 1977. From Stern's front door, a glimpse to the left will reveal the cherished occupants of his six-acre ranch in the distance.

"When you see a horse and there's a sense of balance about their body and the way they move, it's something you can't really define. Sure you can see if one has better conformation, but it goes beyond that. Good horsemen will look at a horse and there's a feeling in the way the horse carries itself. There are some well-bred horses that have almost flawless conformation that can't outrun a chicken," Stern laughs. "Yet we'll see others with not so great conformation that have this ability, this desire. It's spirit and essence, and you see the same in musicians. I know a lot of very, very accomplished, very proficient musicians that hit all the right notes, that seem to play in tune; the rhythm is right, but there's an inner essence that's missing. Maybe it comes from other things. It's also a desire and a hunger, I think. When you see a racehorse that wins, they know when they come in first. It's the same thing in music, you know when you're on."

Stern stops to point out a hummingbird suspended in midair as he walks outdoors toward the barn. "When I perform, there's a moment when you start where you feel this connection with your audience. You know when you're in tune with that audience and that they feel, what you feel in the music. I think there is something similar in the horses, when they know that they're giving their all. There's a strong desire in some horses to be first, to win, to please." The violinist cites a handsome gray colt with a white blaze, who approaches the paddock fence the minute Stern arrives. "He has such a desire to please. When we let him out with the other horses, he wants to be in front. It's just an amazing thing."

Recently weaned, the colt's cordial behavior is typical of the five to eight foals raised each year within eyesight of the musician's home. "We enjoy our size. We can give our horses very individual attention," remarks Stern, who maintains a cap on the ranch's horse population through an annual "distilling" process to keep the number in check. At tops, there are thirty-five to forty horses prior to one of the major sales. "We're 'market breeders,' which means we primarily breed our horses for the Quarter Horse race market," explains Stern. Indicating her picture on the wall of the barn, he proudly notes that a yearling filly named Hey Baby Hey recently fetched $50,000 at a major sale in Oklahoma City, Oklahoma. "One year we ranked fiftieth in the nation as a breeder. With a small herd, that is really amazing. We were competing with ranches with several hundred head."

Standings aside, Stern admits, "The hardest thing is selling them, but even if we sell them, I sort of feel like we're the parents. They might get married to somebody else, but they'll always be our kids and we follow them and we'll go to their races, even though another owner owns them. We keep in close communication usually with most of the people that purchase our horses."

Poised for Patience

Born in the Bronx, New York, Stern had little exposure to horses for years after his initial encounter when he was around nine months and a man with a pony and camera showed up to take pictures of the neighborhood kids. The rapport was instant when Stern's parents put him in the saddle. "They told me they couldn't get me off. I just entwined my fingers in that pony's mane and that began my love of horses," he describes. "As a teenager, I was a concert violinist so I didn't have too much time for many activities, but my brother and I would go to rent stables and ride. That was about my entire experience with horses," says Stern.

Stern's dog reconnected him to horses permanently during his twenties. Long before doggie day camps became fashionable, the violinist took his Samoyed to a nearby ranch, instead of a boarding kennel, whenever he left town on concert tours—along with a stock of roast chicken for the dog's meals. The violinist's love of animals so impressed the rancher that she recommended Stern to a young equestrian bound for college who was looking for a good home for her horse. When Stern purchased a Quarter Horse for his next mount, he discovered a passion for the breed.

"There are almost two distinct breeds in the Quarter Horse— the working cattle type and the racehorse type, which are more infused with Thoroughbred blood for speed." Involvement with pleasure horses and show horses increasingly gave way to Stern Ranch, Ltd.'s focus on breeding and racing.

"I've studied dressage and I used to break all our horses and do the initial training on them," remarks Stern, who invented and patented a bitless bridle called the Donal Horse Perfector that was even sold behind the Iron Curtain in Russia during the Cold War.

Stern delights in describing his novel approach to relaxing horses—singing. Although an accomplished graduate of the Juilliard School of Music, Stern was never much of a singer. "I can hear everything in my ear; I can hear what I want, but what comes out of my throat is something completely different," he explains. Nevertheless, the horses like it.

"Usually it's 'Home on the Range,'" laughs Stern, who finds his equine charges especially responsive to his serenades the first time the blacksmith comes to trim their hooves. "I start holding them and I sing to them and somehow, I think it calms them. My wife Patricia jokingly says that they probably stand still hoping I'll stop singing," he adds. "Whatever way, it works."

From a man whose romance with the violin has led to triumphs from Carnegie Hall to the most lauded symphonies around the world, Stern's candor is refreshing.

In for the Long Haul

"To get into breeding and horses, it's a long-term commitment," says Stern. "Once you've got a mare and you select the stallion, it's an eleven-month gestation until the horse is born. It's three, four years, or longer until you start seeing some revenue for a racehorse. You can't take a young horse and put him in a show arena right away either. I think this has been a good lesson for our family as well. We're such a hurry-up society, I think it's better to retrench sometimes. We bred in the year 2003 for horses that we're not going to see run until 2007 or beyond."

From a family standpoint, the Stern's long-time horse involvement has wrought other benefits. "It's helped us raise our three daughters, Adina, Aura, and Shereen. In their early teenage years, they don't know quite whether they're young girls, or young women, and there's always the boy thing lurking out there. We found that it really helped us a lot when we got our daughters involved in performance horse showing," he explains. Horses also helped diffuse teenage disappointments. "Naturally, being a good parent, we want to know where they are at all times, and when we told them they couldn't go to that party or that sleepover because we didn't think it was an entirely appropriate affair, instead of getting furious at us, they'd go out and talk to their horses about all their problems and the horses would console them," he adds. "Horses have also helped our son Shawn keep focused and do better in school. He is still seriously involved with horses to this day as a young adult. It seems that boys have more of a tendency to stay involved and remain serious about horses their entire lives when started young."

Common Denominators

The sun is approaching high noon in a clear blue sky as a breeze blows lightly. Stern realizes the time. "We have a motto on our ranch, 'Breed the best and forget the rest.' We'll sacrifice to go to the finest stallion with our mares," he remarks.

"There are a great many parallels between doing anything in a finite excellent degree—whether it's music, architecture, or whatever your endeavor," remarks Stern. "What makes a Stradi-varius a Stradivarius is an incredible mystery. Here this man lived in the late sixteen, early seventeen hundreds in Italy, where all around him were hundreds of other violin makers. All had the same basic ingredients, the same woods, the same varnishes, etcetera. What made this man, and maybe one or two others, so much better and more incredible than the rest?" asks Stern. "We've analyzed the instruments, done all sorts of scientific tests on the varnish, the woods, and everything else, and we really don't know what this secret ingredient was." Maybe it's the same illu-sive essence that exists in legendary horses.

◠ TRY THIS

Play a game of Virtual Racehorse Trainer. Only first, you have to make it. Your task is to create an at-home board game using poster board, multicolored index cards, and dice. (First-grade level craft skills are required—you just have to print.) Divide the index cards into separate colors for each category: Horse in Training, Training Challenges, Owner Issues, Trainer Traits.

Now grab that felt marker and get busy. For Horse in Training, list one racehorse name per card. Remember, you may have more than one horse in training. (Miniature horse models can substitute for cards.) Now indulge your imagination with Training Challenges—one challenge per card. These can include a wide range of challenges such as: fast, slow, lazy, lameness problem, spooky, drifts to right, breaks from starting gate well, gives it everything she's got. Also assign a point value to each (i.e., plus or minus one to five points). Shuffle and place face down. Proceed to Owner Issues. Again list one issue along with a point value per card. These may include considerations like: just loves the ambiance, only in it for the money, poor loser, sends horse to another trainer because it lost, offers to buy the horse of your choice at upcoming sale and wants you to train it, thinks everything you do is perfect. Trainer Traits—once again list items that will help or hinder your efforts at the track, giving each one a point value. Some possible traits (include the pros and cons) may include: reads horses well, Trainer of the Year Award, forgets to scratch horse from race, communication skills need improvement.

Now turn the poster board into your game board. Draw an oval track with plenty of lines to create squares for each move. Position horses at the starting gate. Shuffle each deck of issue cards. Roll the dice, move accordingly, and then draw a card from each pile and adjust your position. (Yes, you could be further behind than where you started, or you could find your horse setting a new track record.)

When you're ready to learn more about the largest horse breed association in the world visit the AQHA Web site at *www.aqha.com*. With fans around the planet, the American Quarter Horse is bred to excel in a wide variety of equine talents—from cutting to trail riding and reining, to racing. Among numerous outreach efforts to promote the breed worldwide, AQHA periodically sponsors test rides (on horseback!) to get new riders in the saddle on a Quarter Horse.

Chapter Nine

Responsibility
. . . on course with commitment

There are only so many truths in the universe and they have an incredibly beautiful application in almost every circumstance . . .

—Randy Rieman

THE FOUR-BEAT PATTERN OF hooves on pavement echoes in the background as Dr. Billy Bergin answers his cell phone. Two miles inland on the Big Island of Hawaii, the arid landscape looks more like Arizona or New Mexico than a tropical paradise. As he rides along the road on the back of a three-year-old gelding, the Hawaiian-born veterinarian talks with a caller thousands of miles away. Named for his grandfather, who moved from Cork County, Ireland, to Honolulu in 1888, Bergin is a repository of Island history and local legends. For twenty-five of his thirty-six years in veterinary medicine, Bergin worked with the Parker Ranch, one of the oldest and largest cattle ranches in the United States, encompassing some 175,000 acres of the Big Island. Bergin instantly responds to the phone caller's inquiry with the name of a horseman and friend, the former head trainer at Parker Ranch who is now ensconced in New Mexico. The veterinarian, author, and historian adds, "He's a prince of a person."

The Spirit of Stewardship

Randy Rieman looks every ounce a born-in-the-saddle cowboy with his thick, bushy moustache, crystal clear eyes, and wide-brimmed hat. A man who makes his living starting and training young horses—plus teaching horsemanship and ranch roping clinics around the country—Rieman worked at the Parker Ranch for nearly nine years before making his home in Lamy, New Mexico, about fifteen miles outside of Santa Fe.

"I really started my cowboy career at a late age compared to what most people would think a typical cowboy might do. Although I had a passion for it from the time I was a kid, I never got to express that passion until I was a young adult, twenty-one years old," says Rieman. "I just had a fascination with horses and cowboy things—hats and boots and everything that went along with it."

Born in Iowa, Rieman grew up along the Mississippi River in Illinois, a short distance north of the Missouri milieu that inspired Mark Twain's classic adventure tale, *Tom Sawyer*. After a trip to Montana at seventeen, Rieman's own life adventure set sail, "always in pursuit of horsemanship," he explains.

"I didn't really get to be on horseback that much until I was a teenager and then it was very scattered," he remembers. The attraction, however, was irresistible. Part way through college Rieman saddled up his dreams for good and moved to Montana, his home for the next fifteen years. His path continued through Nevada and California before reaching the Parker Ranch in Hawaii. "I got jobs on ranches with some pretty good horsemen who began to teach me the art of handling livestock and getting into the horse psyche," says Rieman, who counts individuals like Bryan Neubert, Joe Walter, and Billy Askew among his mentors. For Rieman, the equine lifestyle became synonymous with a broader perspective.

"Horses are a part of creation. I believe they were, just like us, created beings and that they were created for a purpose—as were we. We're all part of a whole. If we can function in a spirit of stewardship, then we're probably less likely to be egotistical, or prideful, and possibly more interested in bringing out the best of the animal. That might mean backing off and sacrificing the championship. It might be something as simple as just not trying to use a horse that's not suited for a particular purpose." Rieman contemplates, "We have a responsibility to deal with the horse in a manner that respects his value. We're called not so much to ownership but stewardship."

Yet, many scenarios are diametrically opposed. "A lot of people use everything around them as a trophy to promote themselves," he notes. "A lot use the horse for whatever they're lacking in their own lives. You've seen it a hundred times in every setting. You've seen great riders override the horse. You've seen poor riders abusing the animal because their pride got in the way, or maybe they're blaming their own inadequacies on the animal. That sadly, is what gets in the way a lot of times," says Rieman. "The human ego usually doesn't fit the horse well. However, some people do appreciate the horse for what it is and they seem to be more willing to make adjustments that fit the horse, instead of insisting the horse always fit them."

He adds, "There's no doubt that the rider needs to be in control, but the horse has a point of view also and it's valid. As a rider, if you're not aware of that point of view and respectful of it, then you're not going to be real successful on the long term."

Rieman emphasizes a key point. "For me, as a Christian believer, I trust the Scriptures and the Scriptures of the Bible call us to stewardship, not ownership. The great verse that everyone quotes, 'The cattle on a thousand hills belongs to the Lord.' Well, the horses belong to him and so do we and so do the things we have. My wife isn't mine, she's been loaned to me by the Lord. I'm called to be a steward as her husband. I have certain responsibilities. Same with my finances, same with the horse, if that's what I'm stewarding. I see it more as I've been loaned these privileges on a temporary basis. They're gifts. To me, the horse is one of those gifts."

A Clear Commitment

An accomplished cowboy poet, Rieman has performed publicly for twenty years. His gift for expressing feelings and thoughts is as readily observed in a clinic setting as in presentations of his own works, generally horse-related, such as his CD "Where the Ponies Come to Drink." But it's not a poetry recitation when Rieman broaches horses with a flow of words.

"When you approach a horse, do it with a sense of respect," he articulates. "I don't get on a horse without praying. I ask God for discernment and wisdom, for insight beyond my experience, so I can handle that animal in a way that fits him or her the best, and that I can make it a productive and safe horse for someone else to ride." Rieman succinctly explains, "It's not just my safety that I'm concerned with. I've been given a responsibility by horse owners. They've trusted me with an animal that I want to be sure of when it goes to them. I realize that my responsibility only goes so far, but as far as it goes, I'm willing to use every means at my disposal—my intellect, my physical body, and my spiritual commitment to produce as good a horse as possible and as safe a horse as possible."

Rieman speaks with total candor on how this fits in the context of his personal beliefs. "For me, I can't separate out my Christianity from the horsemanship," he remarks. "When I speak of being a Christian, it's not a doctrine that I adhere to or a set of rules. It's a relationship with the Living Christ. So it's not a religion. It's a relationship and it permeates every aspect of my life. There's nothing I do that doesn't enter into it. That includes horses."

Also, there's another element. "It is a constant awareness and a commitment and recommitment, if you will, on a regular basis—moment-by-moment, day-by-day. It's not something you do on Sunday, it's not something you talk about and then forget. If I left that part of my horsemanship out, I would be leaving out the most valuable part of what I am because in my opinion, we're just spiritual beings having a human experience." Rieman describes the horse-oriented clinics he conducts in a similar vein. They are "problem solving clinics," he notes.

Adversary to Ally

"Many of the people who come to my clinics are at a pretty minimal level of accomplishment. That's one of the reasons they're there. That doesn't include everybody. Some people are quite accomplished and they're just adding to their arsenal," comments Rieman. "People are sometimes shocked, sometimes baffled, and sometimes get real emotional (during clinics), because what seemed so insurmountable a half hour or an hour ago changes from a seemingly unapproachable adversary to almost a gentle, approachable animal." He elaborates, "I use the word adversary a lot at clinics. You have to present information to the horse in a nonadversarial way. It's not by any means passive, but as soon as you act like an adversary, the horse perceives you as one. Sometimes it's based on past experience—you're a human, they had a bad experience with a human, and they put you in that adversarial category right away."

Hearing Rieman delve into his subject matter one could picture him as a counselor or therapist, were it not for his equine calling. "Although the horse is not as complex as the human mentally, they are quite sensitive and go through what we humans go through in similar settings," he describes. "When we feel encroached upon, we want to flee, we want to avoid. If we feel pushed, we want to resist, we want to push back. When we discover someone truly has our best interest at heart, we begin to soften and tolerate and when we're convinced of that, we'll actually begin to yield and participate. A horse goes through many of those same things."

Clinics might double as a personal growth forum for horse and human. "When the information is presented in the correct manner that fits the horse, I think what often happens is you are able to override that flight instance and get the horse even curious," explains Rieman. "Horses go through several phases. The first phase is avoidance, the second phase is actually resistance. They cross the barrier back and forth. Sometimes, it's hard to tell which one is happening, but it goes from avoidance to resistance to tolerance to acceptance. If you're good and you're experienced, you can get beyond that into real mutual pleasurable interaction," Rieman continues. "Unfortunately, a lot of people don't get past the mechanical part, the tolerance part. They don't get to those other places, where the horse and rider start to really enjoy one another."

Rieman grows reflective, "What amazes me is that the horse serves mankind in just about anything you ask him to. You can put him in a mine, you can put him in a war, you can make him haul a wagon across the country, you can jump over a fence, you can swim through water, you can put a saddle on his back and rope another prey animal and he'll stand there and hold it for you. If that isn't the spirit of servitude, I can't imagine what is."

The Perks of Partnership

Since returning to the mainland, Rieman's connection with Hawaii's horse community has continued and even expanded. Summers are spent in the Islands, starting colts for ranches and holding clinics for the public. He's also worked with the Honolulu Mounted Police, a new addition to Waikiki in recent years.

"When you teach the horse how to expand its comfort zone in little mini-crises, it's a great way to establish a bond and communication," recalls Rieman. "We did lots of things to help the officers get a better sense of what's coming with the horse so they can be proactive in their riding instead of reactive—walking over tarps, in between scary objects, up to flares, simulating circumstances where there was aggression, whatever." Besides crowd control, Honolulu Mounted Police patrol the parks and beach—no doubt causing some sun worshipers to put their Mai Tais down.

"A lot of people are very fearful of the horse because it is a large animal with potential hazard attached to it, but when that animal responds in a positive way to its interaction with the human, a special thing takes place," reflects Rieman. For him personally, the impact has been significant.

"Horses have improved my people skills and they've improved my awareness and my powers of observation," Rieman acknowledges. "Every horse is different every day and every horse is different from every other horse. If you're going to work with large numbers of horses, which I've been fortunate to do, and you accomplish that in a really wide variety of environments, there's a constant challenge every day. You can't take it for granted, you can't get complacent, you can't get lazy. You are challenged to think and be completely in the moment. Horses don't carry a watch, they don't read a calendar, they don't know what sign they were born under. What's happening is happening right now and that's the most relevant thing in their lives. That's been a very vibrant circumstance in my life. I appreciate that they have provided that," he adds.

Meanwhile, they've provided lessons in reading unspoken cues. "We get so hooked on verbiage as people," comments Rieman. "I don't believe there's any deceit in an animal. The horse is totally honest. When they act a certain way, it's the truth, so you have to observe and you have to alter your behavior to fit the situation. Your life literally depends on it when you're starting young horses and you're cowboying."

Concurrently, his human insights have also benefited. "I have a tendency to notice when someone's distraught or when someone's upset, or when there's something bad about to take place. With horses, you have to be watching out for what's taking place in a little while, not always what just happened. Kind of like feeling the tremor before the quake," explains Rieman. The nuance of a muscle first tensing can convey volumes, if noticed.

A Matter of Motives

"There are things that bring people together. The spirit in us recognizes the spirit in others," Rieman discusses. "That is not something that's just for Christians. Horse people can spend just a few minutes together and you know that there's a common spirit there. I think in any person who spends a lot of their life with horses, there's a depth that the common, uninitiated just don't have."

Recollecting a film he made on the late Bill Dorrance (an influential California horseman who rode until a year before his death at ninety-three) brings Rieman's comments home. "I originally was going to do just a straight documentary on Bill, but he didn't really think that had any value," Rieman says, with an incredulous tone in his voice. "He said, 'We need to do something that people can get some good out of. Let's teach them to make a reata (lariat),' 'cause Bill loved to braid rawhide. He taught me how," notes Rieman, who directed and produced the ensuing "Four Strands of Rawhide." The two-hour film features Dorrance relating horse stories and circumstances about his life; half is devoted to the art of reata-making he so loved. "Bill was one of those truly humble people who was always 100 percent himself in every circumstance," remembers Rieman. "He was eighty-nine when we did the film."

It's hours past sunset in Lamy, New Mexico, and the brisk air hints of winter to come as Rieman and his wife walk into the house after a full day's ranch roping clinic. The horses are fed and settled in long before the couple digs into a waiting pizza. As if on cue, the phone rings. Just a few questions about when Rieman worked at the Parker Ranch. Might he have any final words about the equine world and stewardship?

Rieman answers, "I think it gets down to motives. Why are you engaging in interaction with the animal? Is it simply your own self-promotion or is there something else? Is there a passionate enjoyment or concern for the animal itself? Is there an appreciation for what the horse has to offer—whether he's a world champion Thoroughbred racehorse or a Shetland pony that an eleven-year-old girl rides?" The horseman concludes, "If you can appreciate the horse for that particular thing that he's serving—be it a draft horse, a jumper, a cow pony, whatever—I think you're getting closer to the kind of stewardship that we're called to."

The Pace of Patience

In 2000, Jennifer Nice earned a coveted spot on the United States Equestrian Team (USET) endurance team after months of preparation and miles in the saddle. Five days before departure for the championships in France, her horse came up lame and Nice withdrew from the competition and gave up her place on the team.

"When I'm not riding, or I'm separated from my horses for any length of time, I feel a huge void," says Nice, who officially logged her first fifty-mile ride in 1989 and has racked up around 5,000 miles of endurance events since. "I started as a jumping kid, got into Quarter Horses, and then Arabians," explains Nice, who worked at David Murdock's Ventura Farms in Thousand Oaks, California, in the early 1980s. "I basically burned out on showing and discovered endurance at the same time."

Born in a military family, Nice grew up moving every two years. She remembers books as the inspiration for her childhood interest in horses. "I had a small paperback of all the horse breeds. I lived with that book," she recalls. "It was dog-eared. I would always mark my favorite horse and I changed my mind frequently."

Whether by accident or design, Nice's adult equestrian interests have often dovetailed literary pursuits. One year after her USET plans were waylaid, Nice moved to Abu Dhabi for two years to work for the President of the United Arab Emirates, H. H. Sheikh Zayed Bin Sultan Al Nahyan. "I split my time between editing two magazines and training endurance horses," describes Nice, who had up to eighteen horses in training at a time. When she returned to the United States in 2003, Nice took over the editorship of the *Paint Horse Journal*, the magazine of the thriving Fort Worth, Texas—based breed association.

"I am attracted to the 'problem children' horses—the horses that no one else wants or can ride," says Nice, who juggles work demands with assorted endurance competitions. "I get a lot of satisfaction working with a horse that has issues and turning them into successful endurance horses. I feel like I'm giving them a chance that no one else might. I feel a greater sense of accomplishment in bringing such a horse along and finishing an endurance race than I do taking a superior horse and winning." She asks, "What's the fun in winning when you know you can win? I would rather finish on a horse that I don't know will finish. That takes a lot of patience."

Of her three current horses (two are purebred Arabians), Air Force is a case in point. "When I got him, no one could catch him, touch his face, or his legs. He was nearly impossible to ride, very spooky, and completely lacking confidence. He's come a long way in less than a year."

The key to managing two time-intensive callings? Nice responds, "I enjoy my job and I love to ride, so it doesn't seem like a lot to take on. Sometimes my job prevents me from riding, but it all works out. I just set my goals so that they are attainable."

ᛜ Try This

If you are unfamiliar with "natural horsemanship" practices, find out about horse expos in your area. Equine Affaire (*www.equine affaire.com*), which is held in several locations across the country, includes an opportunity to see numerous top clinicians along with the admission price. These and other "horse whisperers" tour the country frequently. Area tack stores, equestrian centers, horse publications, and the Internet are good sources for determining who may be in your area. If you have the budget to travel, try attending a clinic given by the person of your choice in another part of the country (or world). Often, the organizer will suggest accommodations and make a point of welcoming you into a ready-made group of new horse friends. Note: Although many individuals who offer horsemanship clinics choose to avoid the moniker "horse whisperer," using it will ensure your intent is not misunderstood if you are new to equestrian lingo.

Prefer to stay at home and learn rawhide reata braiding while hearing stories from the late Bill Dorrance? Pick up a video at *www.ranch2arena.com* and plan accordingly. Traditionally, these are braided to a seventy-foot length or longer! And should you wake at night lured by the thought of Hawaiian trade winds, ride the Internet to Parker Ranch at *www.parkerranch.com* and read about "paniolos," Hawaii's cowboys.

Chapter Ten

Reflection
... the equine mirror

Horses represent the other part of self, the child-like innocence and openness to all things new, what we want to be. When we are open to them, they bring us back to our deeper self . . .

—Mother Hildegard George

AN HOUR OFF THE coast of Washington by ferry, Mother Hildegard George tends to the llamas on the smallest of the San Juan Islands with regular boat service—Shaw Island—while contemplating prizes for each child participating in an upcoming 4-H club event. A Roman Catholic nun and member of a Benedictine monastery for women, Our Lady of the Rock, George and her counterparts run a 300-acre farm on the secluded island, which has a total population of about 150 people. Devoted to preserving rare breeds of animals, the nuns oversee Kerry cattle to Cotswold sheep in the pastoral setting. Lush gardens of flowers, vegetables, and herbs help them to be largely self-sufficient.

"We don't raise horses, but a logger on the island has a couple of Percherons and Belgians that he boards on our property so we get to look out and see these magnificent huge creatures. They kind of cohabitate with the cows and the llamas and everybody gets along," says George, who holds a doctorate degree in child and adolescent psychology and founded the island's 4-H club.

Leading with Love

"I rode most of my life," remarks George, who's been a featured speaker at educational equine events in the United States and Canada. Her keynote address on "The Spirit of the Horse and the Spirituality of the Child" at the 2003 Alberta Horse Breeders and Owners Conference, attracted widespread attention. "One of the things I like to stress is, while the horse gives the child many opportunities to shine, it is the relationship between the child and the animal that's important, not the ribbons or the trophies this team may produce," notes George. "We need to pass on the joy of riding, the unconditional love the animal gives us over any desire to be first. This is something I really strive for with my 4-H kids, that they love their animals above all things and not worry about all the ribbons and trophies they can possibly win." (While Shaw Island's 4-H club is known for llamas, not horses, the emphasis remains the same.)

George began receiving invitations to equine conferences and events after conducting workshops for Canadian humane societies several years in a row. Her talks consistently draw curious audiences from considerable distances. "I just think it's so important that kids really develop that relationship with their animal. It's one of those things in our society that's not happening—developing relationships—because we're so competitive about everything. From the time kids start preschool they have to be competitive about whatever they're doing. I don't think that's what the animal is all about," reflects George, who was raised in Santa Monica and Pasadena at a time she describes, "when Los Angeles was still a beautiful place to grow up." Horses entered her life at an early age.

"My grandfather was a cowboy, a real cowboy. He had a large cattle ranch in Colorado and I think he was still riding when he died at seventy-eight," recalls George. "The interesting thing is my mother's youngest brother was kicked in the head by a horse and killed when he was ten, so my mother had a real hard time with us on horses. The amazing thing is she still rode. My father loved to take trips up in the High Sierras and places where you could only get in by horseback. She'd go with him, God bless her. I was put on my first horse, probably by my grandfather, when I was four and the story goes that I fell off and I was screaming. My mother nearly passed out at the fence watching me, but the only reason I was screaming is I wanted back on the horse. I loved riding. I think girls go through a stage where horses are number one in your life," comments George.

Once a trainer for the Delta Society, a nonprofit leader in research and applications of the animal-human bond, George has been at the forefront of animal-assisted therapy with children. "Girls and horses—wow! There's probably no group in our society, from zero to one hundred, that are more difficult to work with than teenage girls. I think it's hard for them at certain ages to really find a passion in things, but when they do, boy, they really latch on. I think it's something we need to address when we deal with teenage girls, even in normal development—if teens can be said to be a normal time for anyone. I think it gives them an outlet to put this passion in a very positive light."

George continues, "The nurturing, I think, is very important for girls. It gives them a chance to love something in a very positive manner, not 'throw it away too early,' if you know what I mean. I would pretty much guarantee you that most girls who are passionate about horses are not into drugs and sex and things like that because their energies are going in a very positive direction. Young men, the same thing. I'm not sure we're educating kids properly in our society. We cram them into classrooms at an age where the hormones, testosterone, and everything's all over the place. I think horses are a very healthy outlet on a lot of levels."

There is another aspect to horses that is not found in other animals—elephants and camels notwithstanding.

"The thing about a horse is you're actually on it, so it's almost like you become one with the horse. Studies have shown that the gait of the horse mimics our own gait. A lot of children that can't walk or have a hard time walking can actually feel what it must be like when they get on the horse," adds George, who was a consultant to a riding school for the handicapped in the Northwest. "So, I think there's a physiological aspect, but I think there's also a psychological, spiritual aspect. I can certainly remember every time I got on a horse. You just feel like you're ten feet taller than you really are. There's just something noble and regal about horses."

Animal Accessible

The last time George climbed aboard a horse was roughly fifteen years ago on the 160-acre farm campus of Green Chimneys Children's Services and Green Chimneys School in Brewster, New York, where she initiated the therapy program using animals. "They're really one of the pioneers in the world in terms of having animals accessible to the kids practically 24/7 and these, for the most part, are severely abused kids from the inner city of New York. The kind of kids you probably would not want to put an animal in the hands of, and yet the kids are absolutely wonderful," remarks George. Specializing in equine-assisted psychotherapy and equine experiential learning, Green Chimneys provides a wide array of programs to children, adolescents, and families.

"One of the wonderful things at Green Chimneys is every kid gets to ride the horses. They all go off to the county fair and they're in one of the richest counties of the United States. For the most part, they're black and Hispanic kids and boy they come home with the awards! You better believe it. It's quite an amazing program. They all learn English (riding) and they do dressage and learn how to ride bareback with three and four on the horse doing tricks. It takes a little bit of learning to do a lot of this. I think we kind of underestimate kids," comments George. The Benedictine nun has several published works on interventions in therapy for children and adolescents, child abuse, domestic violence, and animal abuse.

She offers a candid perspective on learning. "I think that we adults love to always be in the limelight and are not always wanting to let kids take responsibility that they really are the best educators of each other," considers George. "They learn from each other. They certainly learn by watching us, but they actually learn a lot faster [from their peers], especially the kids who have been abused by adults so much they don't want to trust adults anymore. They'll trust one another and they trust the animals." George adds, "In the three years that I was at Green Chimneys, I never ever saw any kind of deliberate animal abuse."

Child Whispering

Every time a child is labeled, a door closes, George contends. "I'm afraid all we do in our society is label everybody. Then somebody comes along and they pick up on whatever, the evaluation, and we're labeled and they don't really take the time to get to know us. I'm afraid too many children are going through life like this." The irony of the situation bears examination. "We love diversity in our society and yet if a child's got one little thing that's different from the next group of children, we say there's something wrong with them. I have a really hard time with that," she reflects.

Shaw Island is a mere seven-square-miles of landmass surrounded by sea, but its occupants distill truths as big as the universe.

"It's a really wonderful place to raise kids. They just don't have this incredible competitive edge where they lose sight of what it's all about and I think that's really, really important. The last couple of years we've had fifteen kids in the 4-H program between the two islands. I'm the llama superintendent as well, so I'm the one that has to come up with all the awards. I make sure that every kid gets a major award."

George consults and teaches for American Humane Association and the Washington State University School of Veterinary Medicine, in addition to her myriad of duties and devotional commitments at the gated monastery overlooking the water. "There are a lot of books out there about people whispering to horses and they say that the best training is based on collaboration and sensitivity. We have to have a lot of heart and patience in what we do," George reflects. "To me, we've got to do the same with children. We've got to do a lot more whispering to children than we do."

The Stable of Symbols and Signs

Jacqueline Welles lives the bicoastal equivalent of yin and yang, splitting her time between upstate New York and Southern California. A retired Human Services professor and Certified Gestalt therapist turned psychic, Welles recalls the vivid significance of Pegasus in a dream preceding a cross-country journey to Los Angeles, when she established a West Coast base well over a decade ago. "Pegasus represented being able to go anywhere, do anything," notes Welles, who's worked extensively with dream symbolism for thirty years.

"In most dream interpretation, the horse is the body," explains Welles, whose glistening gray hair, reminiscent of a sliver fox, accentuates her electric green eyes. "In Gestalt dream inter-pretation, you would have to go through the steps and determine what it would be in your own individual mind at that time. It might change over the years. But when you buy dream books and check out the interpretations, they almost always say the horse is your physical body. I pretty much could verify that from hearing thousands of dreams over the years," adds Welles, who holds a master's of science degree in psychology, along with credentials as a certified hypnotherapist and rebirther.

No stranger to the literal ramifications of horses in the flesh, the native New Yorker describes a poignant memory from her own early experiences. "I lived out in the country, so you were always getting popped onto the back of somebody's horse for two minutes here, three minutes there," Welles notes. The description of her first serious riding attempt at age twelve prompts an unabashed laugh.

"One of our neighbors up the road had gotten a mustang during the very start of the adoption programs and there wasn't a lot of guidance on what to do. For reasons completely unknown to me, they fenced in two acres that went up a hill into the woods and built a beautiful little stable. Then, without thinking 'this is a wild horse,' they brought it home, let it out of the horse trailer, and essentially nobody ever saw it again. It would come down to eat in the stable, but every time the people would try to shut the doors, the damn thing would just come roaring out, and refuse to eat at the stable for another week."

Undaunted, the budding equestrian devised a plan of her own. Welles remembers, "I had read *The Black Stallion* and I was really influenced by the thought that if I could make friends with this horse, it would just let me on its back and we would ride like the wind. Well, I started sneaking up through the woods and giving him apples and carrots. I really did make friends with the horse. So one day, I finally climbed a tree and got on its back and I darn near got killed." Welles describes the carnage, which was anything but the image conjured by the novel. "I was able to hang on for a little while, but it was bucking like crazy and tried to scrape me off on trees," remembers Welles, who attempted the feat bareback with no bridle, just like the literary inspiration. "I finally flew off—disaster," she remarks. Plus there was the sobering realization: "It was not like the book."

One could easily understand had Welles's horse interests stopped then, but she's rarely passed up opportunities to ride in the years since and continues an affinity for the animal. Perhaps unsurprisingly, her clientele as a psychic includes a number of individuals involved with horses.

"When you get on a horse, you're weightless essentially and the horse is doing all the work. You're moving through the air very freely. I get the same sensation on roller coasters and things like that," notes Welles, whose immersion in various spiritual traditions—including Taoism—stretches back to her teaching days at Corning Community College in Corning, New York—and even before. "I honestly wonder sometimes whether very, very spiritual people tend to have more of an interest in horses because of that ability to feel very weightless," she reflects. "It's also a partnership. I'm always very grateful to a horse for carrying me and making me feel like that."

Straight from the Cinematherapy Corral

Gary Solomon, M.S.W., Ph.D., doesn't own horses or ride them. Many days they never enter his mind. But sometimes a film like *The Horse Whisperer* will end up in one of his books.

"Movies are the guiding mythology of the United States today. Put that in the world of psychology and it works very well," remarks Solomon, a psychotherapist, educator, and author, who coined the term Cinematherapy and wrote the first book on the subject of using movies to help deal with life's problems. "The key to this process is prescribing the right movie for the right problem," notes Solomon, whose seminal book *The Motion Picture Prescription: Watch This Movie and Call Me in the Morning* earned international media attention and catapulted him into the spotlight.

"One of the most difficult things to do as a therapist is to help people understand concepts like denial, codependency, and addiction," remarks Solomon, a professor of psychology at Community College of Southern Nevada in Henderson, a Las Vegas suburb. "Dramatic film images can evoke emotion and stimulate the type of immediate response that rarely happens in conversation."

Solomon explains how the 1998 movie *The Horse Whisperer* starring Robert Redford—and some of the most talented movie horses in the business—holds such therapeutic potential years after its box office debut. "When the accident occurs and the horse and the child are scarred, we see a wonderful example of what it is like to be scarred inside, by looking at the horse's external scar," describes Solomon, former director of Arizona Family Counseling and Education in Phoenix and before that, Portland's prominent Oregon Psychotherapy Consortium. "And the healing process that takes place, occurs with both of them simultaneously. The girl is withdrawn. She rejects everybody— her family, friends, her horse. Everybody. So does the horse. And in the process of the healing comes this emergence of a new horse, or a healed horse, as well as a healed child, and they come together again at the end."

The "father of Cinematherapy" continues. "Now, is this idealistic? Absolutely. Is this the way we would like therapy to go? You bet! Is it the way that things happen in the real world? Probably not. It's an event that we'd like to think takes place in therapy, but in therapy, we can't see the external scars. With this particular movie, *The Horse Whisperer*, we can see the external scar," explains Solomon, who holds master's degrees in public health and social work, plus doctorate degrees in psychology and social work. (He was also once lead singer for the rock n' roll group Strawberry Alarm Clock.)

"Now, there are other factors that take place in this movie—this man can speak to horses by understanding horse language, if you will, by body movement, which is primarily the way he communicates. The other issue is the potential affair that the mother has with the horse whisperer, but the conflict there becomes what is right and what is wrong. What is the moral issue with respect to that and of course morally, she does the right thing," concludes Solomon.

The California-born author of three Cinematherapy books reflects, "Hollywood has been making healing movies for years without knowing it." Consequently, films like *The Horse Whisperer* can profoundly touch even armchair equestrians. "Sometimes the answers to life's problems are in the movies," adds Solomon. And sometimes, the messengers are horses.

☾ TRY THIS

Help yourself to a mirror of choice for a round of inner reflection illuminated by the horse. If you choose to go to the Cinematherapy corral and sample the movie route, libraries and neighborhood video stores sometimes carry more obscure horse films (like *Into the West* starring Gabriel Byrne) than larger chains. Visit *www.cinema-therapy.com* before you begin. Gary Solomon advocates watching videos at home (versus going to theaters) and avoiding snacks and refreshments when viewing movies as a therapeutic (versus entertainment) process. Journaling and post-movie discussions come into play as well.

If you're inclined to dream, keep paper and pen by your bed and make notes immediately upon awakening. Key points can be forgotten in less than a minute. Pay attention to your emotions (i.e. sad, happy). Break down the dream with key players and events—like the cast and acts in a play. If a horse is present, be especially sure to record pertinent details. Should animals talk in dreams there may well be added significance. Many bookstores carry a wide selection of books on dream symbols. Often courses on understanding dreams are available through community colleges. Determining the personal significance of symbols can be particularly enlightening. It's like learning a language of your own.

For those who prefer to make reflection a hands-on activity, instead of dreams and movies, visit *www.rockisland.com, www.green chimneys.org,* and *www.deltasociety.org* to see what intrigues you.

Chapter Eleven

Rhythm
. . . hearing the hoofbeat

*What gives life to the living
never dies, though what it
produces does die. What
transforms things never changes,
though what it transforms does change . . .*
—Thomas Cleary

TWO ORNATE GATES SWING OPEN AT THE ENTRANCE TO CASA DE Shenandoah, revealing a tree-lined drive flanked by white-fenced fields of grazing Arabians as a mesmerizing song of peacock calls and horse whinnies echoes across the fifty-two-acre ranch Wayne Newton calls home. Tan, fit, and welcoming, the legendary entertainer stands well over six feet in cowboy boots. He shows little indication of his rigorous six-night-a-week performance schedule at the Stardust Resort & Casino—twenty minutes away, barn-door-to-stage-door, on the Las Vegas Strip. Chairman of the USO Celebrity Circle, Newton often departs within hours of wrapping up his Stardust engagements to perform before troops in locations from the Persian Gulf to Iraq. Homecomings religiously begin with a stop by the barn to see the horses—just like every night after his show.

Tides of Life

"My two loves in life, from the time I can remember, were music and horses, and I couldn't decide which I loved more," says Newton laughing, "I can tell you which afforded the other." For decades Newton has been an entertainment icon—with even a thoroughfare at McCarran International Airport bearing his name. Yet for thirty-eight years, "Mr. Las Vegas" has also been an award-winning horse breeder whose Wayne Newton's Aramus Arabians can be found from Denmark to Australia.

Near the front pasture Newton cradles a two-day-old colt, proudly introducing him to a visitor, as the foal's mother calmly observes from a distance. Reunited, the two join five other mares and foals in the field. Newton is just warming up. Next he grabs the lead rope to a glistening stallion, WN Ibn Ali, who is prancing and snorting, intent on impressing two mares in an adjacent paddock. A few words from Newton and the stallion stands motionless, neck and head perfectly poised, all attention fixed on his owner.

"I'm not a spectator by nature. I have to be involved with them and I have to try to make some contribution to the breed. The Arab horse offers me that," remarks Newton. At last count, there were eighty-five Arabians at Casa de Shenandoah.

Honored with the Breeder of the Year Award in 1996 from the Arabian Professional and Amateur Horseman's Association, his farm has produced national champions in halter and performance across professional, amateur, and youth ranks. Internationally, Newton-bred Arabians have won national championship titles in Canada, Denmark, Germany, Australia, South Africa, and Brazil— including the 2002 Brazilian National Champion Mare, WN Fawn Obsession. Clearly identified by the "WN" carried in their registered names, there's no mistaking a Wayne Newton-bred horse.

Newton's fascination with horses began early, instigated by an uncle with a farm and horses in his home state of Virginia. "I would beg my parents to take me to his farm," he recalls. "The first place that I'd head would be the barn, because I was sure that there was a pony for me. There never was."

In sixth grade, however, the aspiring horseman simply took matters into his own hands, selling his bicycle and his parents' movie camera to buy a foal he'd found at a stable. "Then, I had to explain to my parents not only had I taken their movie camera, but I now had something else that we had to feed," remembers Newton. "So that was my first horse."

Before plunging into Arabians, Newton raised Thoroughbreds and Quarter Horses for a time. "One day I went by this barn in Phoenix and standing in the stall was the most beautiful horse I'd seen in my life. I said to the owner, 'What is that?' and they said, 'That's an Arabian.' I knew I was headed the wrong direction with the other breeds," he recalls. Newton's ensuing passion and devotion to the progress of the Arabian horse worldwide has made him a well-known ambassador for the breed.

"Aramus was the horse that got it all started for me," explains the multitalented entertainer about the namesake for which his Wayne Newton's Aramus Arabians was founded. "He was the horse I just fell in love with, and he won more national championships than any other horse in the history of the breed."

Many of the bloodlines still prevalent in Newton's herd can be traced to Aramus, a stallion imported from Poland, in addition to Spanish and Egyptian lines of Arabians also used in the breeding program.

"Aramus died when he was twelve and just at the height of his career," recalls Newton, his feelings for the stallion still evident. "This is the irony of my life, to a certain extent. Aramus died in January of 1976 and my first daughter was born in July 1976. The horse that was the counterpart to Aramus, Arn-ette Perlane, died in January of 2002, and my second daughter was born in April. So it seems that every time the good man upstairs would take something that meant that much to me, something would come along that would just mean a lot more."

Both Aramus and Arn-ette Perlane are buried on the ranch grounds, still close in spirit, as each spring foal crop brings new legacies to their bloodlines.

Natural Progression

"I make all the decisions as to who's bred to whom, which ones are shown, which ones are kept," says Newton. "One thing I breed into our herd deliberately, and without reservation, is temperament." During the height of foaling season, Newton's work just begins when he returns from his show at the Stardust. "At this ranch, we have foaled to date about 620 babies," he explains. "I do most of the foaling myself."

The foaling barn, with oversized stalls for pregnant mares, includes a special stall that's served as the delivery room for generations of Newton's Arabians.

"It's amazing, particularly the maiden mares that are having their first babies," remarks Newton. "You bring them in that foaling stall and they settle right down. They don't necessarily know why, I don't think, but it's the fact that they were born there and their mothers were born here."

Among the miracles witnessed in the foaling stall, Newton recalls one mare who apparently refused to have her foal while he was on the road. She was nearly a month overdue, uncomfortable, and grouchy when he returned.

"When I got home, I went straight to the barn," Newton recalls. He convinced his wife, Kathleen, to sit in a corner of the foaling stall with him to wait. "The mare came over and she nuzzled around my face and around my ear and went over and laid down and had her baby."

The transformative qualities of such experiences have touched those closest to him.

"My wife loved horses as a child. Then she was injured at a summer camp jumping—the horse stopped, she went over his head, and cut both knees down to the bone. She was afraid of horses from that point on," describes Newton. "When we got married I said, 'Look, we've got to get you over this.' The way I got her through it was she started helping me foal the mares."

Typically, foaling is a family affair in the Newton household, a ritual joined by the head trainer and his wife, with bets wagered—is it a boy or a girl? A night watch person and camera in the stall ensures observation of expectant mares around the clock. Within seconds of the first signs of a foal's arrival, phone calls summon everyone to the barn.

"If I'm not home, of course my people are trained to do the foaling," notes Newton. From day one, foal imprinting is used to establish a bond of trust, which is immediately apparent in behavior.

"Here's a perfect example of it," says Newton as a gregarious colt, WN Fast Lane, displays more interest in his owner than his nearby dam. "He will get in your pocket if you let him."

A Cadence in Common

For all his accomplishments as a performer, Newton's horse breeding operation has opened doors that his musical career couldn't. When his late father, Patrick, was in need of a medical specialist, Newton contacted a renowned international heart surgeon halfway across the country, whom he'd never met, in hope the doctor would take his father on as a patient.

The physician immediately agreed. Newton later learned the doctor did so not because he was a noted entertainer, but because a horse trainer for a royal family overseas (the doctor was treating a member of the family) had said, "Some guy by the name of

Wayne Newton raises the best Arabian horses in the United States."

Newton reflects, "You never know how far-reaching something like that becomes when people have a love for animals and horses. Here, worlds apart, my father needs an operation and the best doctor in the world to do it, luckily, is a horse lover."

Home on His Range

Newton swings into the saddle aboard a handsome, big-bodied gray named WN Lazar and puts the gelding in a slow jog toward the pond in front of his house. Unable to resist, he stops as his beaming little daughter Lauren reaches from her mother's arms to get on the horse with daddy. The Newton passion for horses is clearly implanted in the smiling toddler.

Meanwhile, elsewhere on the ranch, the finishing touches proceed on a new thirty-seven stall barn, complete with office, tack and laundry rooms, grooming stalls, rubber brick floors, and wash racks with hot and cold water. Landscaping, also in process, will add a stream and waterfall, more pastures, and paddocks.

"They're more than just horses, they're special souls," reflects Newton, who has performed live for more than thirty million people (and counting). "No matter what goes on at the club or what goes on in town, or in my career, or anything that happens to one in life, the one place I always found solace was with my horses. They have just been such an inspiration to me."

The Equine Antidote

A day after returning from months in the Czech Republic on a film production, director Martha Coolidge is on the phone at her home in Los Angeles talking horses, while reacquainting herself with the sight of her Paso Finos. The foaling area, a large paddock, is right outside the bedroom window, she notes. Past President of the Directors Guild of America (DGA), Coolidge currently serves as First Vice-President on the National Board of Directors.

"I was sort of raised to be an artist. Then in college I decided I should be a filmmaker and there weren't any women directors," explains Coolidge, a distant cousin of United States president Calvin Coolidge. "Everybody told me it was impossible, but I just went straight ahead and became a film director. But it took everything. It took devotion, moving from city to city, following projects up."

Coolidge began an award-winning professional film career, initially producing and directing documentaries, after graduating from New York University Institute of Film and Television with a master's of fine arts degree. At the helm of diverse film projects—from raucous comedy to drama—she's worked with artists such as Robert Duvall and Jack Lemmon to Geena Davis and Halle Berry. Along the way, Coolidge discovered great talents like Nicolas Cage and Val Kilmer.

"It wasn't until I was thirty-five, that I started really making any kind of money, so I just didn't have an opportunity to think of anything else," remembers Coolidge. "Then when I was in my forties, my mother said to me, 'I'm really surprised that you've not bought a horse. It's so funny, given all the things you wanted in your life.'" The high-powered director comments, "She put the idea in my head."

Born and raised in New Haven, Connecticut, Coolidge's attraction to horses commenced well before she first sat in the saddle, at about six. "I was one of those little girls who loved horses, I sort of worshiped them from afar. I didn't grow up with them," says Coolidge, who began riding at stables near her childhood home and was exposed to both English and Western riding lessons.

"I started drawing horses like crazy, fell in love with *The Black Stallion* books, read everything about horses—all the mythology, Indian lore, cowboy books, everything that I could find—and certainly grew up on Westerns," recalls Coolidge. The long awaited opportunity to indulge her passion arrived at thirteen, when she leased a horse for the summer. She recalls days of riding bareback through woods and fields with other horseback friends with pleasure. "I don't think I was a super great rider, just confident with horses and I felt comfortable with them," says Coolidge. College and the onset of her film career almost permanently sidetracked Coolidge's equestrian pursuits. Even when she moved to California and had friends with horses, the all-engrossing nature of the film business kept even them at arm's length for many years. Coolidge might have lost track of a childhood dream, were it not for a mother's sage advice. The topic of horses resurfaced at a prodigious time.

"This is a really funny story," mentions Coolidge. "I had a child, my son Preston, when I was forty-two. When he was in preschool, I told my friend, 'You've got to donate something to the preschool auction if you want to get [your child] into the kindergarten." Coolidge laughs, "I mean that's LA, right?" The friend, a Paso Fino horse breeder, decided to donate a horse. Primed for the bait (thanks to her mother), Coolidge went to investigate exactly what a Paso Fino was all about, since she'd never heard of the smooth-gaited breed, which initially flourished in Puerto Rico and Columbia centuries ago. Coolidge was soon sold not only on the auction prospect, but on the breed itself.

"I'd been out of the whole thing for so long, but I wasn't a complete fool about buying a horse. I thought well, go ride the horse, see if I like it." The ambiance couldn't have appealed more to a director's eye. "So I went up to this awesome ranch in Agua Dulce, with about 100 Paso Finos. I get on the horse, it's alive! A horse with spirit, and way smoother than anything I'd ever ridden. I rode her a few times and I bought her at the auction."

Getting back into horses proved to be a brand new adventure for the distinguished director. "I was at ease with horses, but I hadn't ridden for so long, I came in a confident lower-intermediate rider," describes Coolidge. "What I found immediately, is they were an incredible antidote to the film business."

Reworking Rhythm, a Hoofbeat at a Time

Coolidge's unplanned foray into the Paso Fino world exposed her to a breed with a natural four-beat gait so rhythmic and smooth, that public exhibitions sometimes feature horseback riders traversing wooden boards on the ground, flanked by microphones, so the distinctive beat of the hooves can be heard. Yet beyond a pattern of hoofbeats, another aspect of rhythm became apparent through her association with the horse.

"I'm a very high-strung, high-energy person," she remarks. "And I am attracted to high-strung, high-energy people and animals—which Paso Finos are, but they're very willing." Coolidge suddenly found herself challenged to truly relax.

"I had to learn to be in the present, because everything about what I do is the future," she explains. "What is the film going to end up like? How do you handle this situation to make it come out? What's your plan for the day? What's your plan for the hour? Is the sun going down? Is it raining? Is somebody sick? It's always pushing against a clock—lots of anxiety and tremendous stress," describes Coolidge, whose many accomplishments include directing *Introducing Dorothy Dandridge* for HBO, for which she garnered a Directors Guild nomination, as well as an Emmy for star Halle Berry.

Coolidge finishes describing her introduction to Paso Finos, "So there I am driving out to Agua Dulce to get on a horse and find that any little tiny thought that I have is reflected right back at me—instantly. I made a huge effort to really understand the horse, understand myself, and open that channel. I'd go out on the trail and I rode for three months, essentially by myself. I just loved it." Horse fever soon took over. After selling her first horse to a friend, Coolidge upgraded to a better one—then bought a stallion and a gelding. "By the end of that year, I owned five and a baby. Then I went so crazy I bought into the business."

With the same gusto that propelled her film career, Coolidge plunged into the thick of things. "I did the right thing by going in with somebody that knew what they're doing. I did the wrong thing by going in too big. After a few years, I ended up managing this ranch with 100 horses on it, everything from electricity bills to trainer bills to vet bills," describes Coolidge. "And this is in my spare time! While I'm raising a family, on the board of the Directors Guild, and having a directing career. It got to the point where it was almost not fun. I learned all about the breed, but God, the more you learn, the more you know how little you know."

What did become clear was the need to regroup, cut back the number of horses she owned, and find a solution amenable to an already fast-paced rhythm of life. A pocket of horse country "in town" not far from Burbank, presented an opportunity for Coolidge to buy her own ranch, where the family now lives on property with their fourteen Paso Finos. They are now just a door, or window, away.

"Just to go out, groom the horse, ride the horse, commune with horses, is for me the single most 'zen' thing I do," comments Coolidge. "I'm not a person with a super-duper amount of patience, but they've taught me. I've learned so much about how we learn from horses."

It's a little more than a decade since the fateful preschool auction that plunged Coolidge back into horses. In that time, she has literally bred equine families and had the chance to observe them. "I've owned four generations of horses and have known enough of their relatives to see traits. I've watched the mares teaching the foals and I just think they have incredible memories. I've seen how fast it happens. How quickly a horse learns something that imprints and it never goes away."

In a business where each visual nuance holds significance on the screen, Coolidge mentions that horses have helped her become more sensitive to reading signs and nonverbal signals. "They have tremendous learning by sight and it's not something people talk about. They can feel anything and they also watch. I ski and a while ago they discovered that if you showed a videotape of a person skiing in perfect form and you just looked at it all the time, you'd ski better. I really feel that horses themselves learn by looking at other horses and observing—not thinking in our sense, but doing and then repetition."

Although film locations sometimes keep Coolidge out of the saddle for days, if not weeks, it's merely a longer pause between the ebb and flow of her equestrian existence. "I've ridden in the Rose Parade and the Fiesta of the Spanish Horse," says Coolidge, who is active in promoting the Paso Fino breed. An avid trail rider, she also competes in local to national horse shows.

"It's not a breed that has an overwhelming presence in California or the West for that matter, but in my opinion, for riding, I don't know why anyone rides anything but a Paso

Fino," comments Coolidge candidly. "That doesn't mean I don't love other horses and don't ride them. I do. Each breed has its own characteristics."

In fact, had she not gotten in the film business, she might have pursued a career in the horse industry, Coolidge admits. "I like them that much," she adds. "But for me, it's very important that horses are not work and I enjoy the work I do."

The gifted director becomes pensive. "I love being away from engines and being with an animal that liberated man into a kind of travel that you couldn't do on foot. I always think of how many thousands of years man has depended on the horse," says Coolidge. "It's like being connected to nature, which makes me feel more whole. It's very transcendental."

⟁ Try This

Get in tune with your own tides of life. Did a childhood dream about horses, or otherwise, fall by the wayside? Ask family and friends about interests and ideas you mentioned well before your teens. (Memory can be deceiving. If you don't believe it, reread a letter or journal ten years later.) Conscious awareness of a forgotten idea may unleash new possibilities.

Are you more the type to rev up for a round of Lunar Horse Revelations? If you are lucky enough to have daily exposure to a horse, this one may be for you! Use a handheld recorder or notebook. Beginning on the new moon, make a single observation per day about the horse you are watching, on something you've not previously considered—this may be a parallel between your personal life and the horse's behavior. Continue this daily until the full moon. Then, and only then, listen or look at what you've recorded or written. You may find some interesting revelations on rhythms and patterns courtesy of the horse.

Internet travelers, for a Web site encounter with the rhythmic Paso Fino, see *www.pfha.org*.

Or, take a virtual visit to Wayne Newton's ranch, Casa de Shenandoah, at *www.waynenewton.com*. Find more details on the Arabian horse at *www.ArabianHorse.org*.

Chapter Twelve

Peace
. . . the unequivocal ambassador

Horses transcend language, culture, and politics . . .
—Elizabeth Kaye McCall

THE MOON FINALLY APPEARED IN THE DARK NIGHT SKY OF WORLD War II–Czechoslovakia as Captain Thomas Melville Stewart piloted a Lipizzaner stallion at a gallop toward a three-foot abatis blocking the road to Hostau. A heartbeat before the surge of equine muscles that would propel the officer over the roadblock toward his destination in German-occupied territory, a warning rang out. "He doesn't jump!" yelled Dr. Rudolph Lessing, a German captain and staff veterinarian enroute to Hostau with

Stewart—the Intelligence Officer for the 42nd Squadron of the United States Army's 2nd Cavalry.

It was too late for Stewart to abort the intended leap over the blockade as he closed his legs against the horse's sides—committed to the course of action already set in motion. Silhouetted by a pale shaft of moonlight, the white stallion gathered himself and surged over the barrier. The horse carried the Captain toward a destination where the opposition of political adversaries proved secondary to horsemen united in an effort to return the famous white Lipizzaners to their home in Austria.

Mission of Horsemen

"The 2nd U.S. Cavalry put a hold on the war for two days while we extracted a sliver of culture for the rest of the world," remembers Louis T. Holz, of Wayne, Pennsylvania, who was a lieutenant during the World War II coup that came to be known as Operation Cowboy. During the mission, the 2nd Cavalry rescued the Lipizzaner stud farm's breeding stock from the German Remount Depot in Hostau, where hundreds of horses were held. "I don't necessarily think everybody else would have recognized the historical and cultural importance of these animals," remarks Holz. "Our leaders did." Both Colonel John Hancock Reed, Commanding Officer of the 2nd Cavalry, and his superior and friend, the 3rd U.S. Army Commander General George S. Patton, were horsemen. (Patton was on the 1912 United States Olympic Equestrian team.)

Before arriving near the border of Germany and Czechoslovakia, the 2nd Cavalry had crossed France, the Rhine River, and Central Germany, witnessing widespread destruction and grisly conditions. The saga that unfolded in the lush tranquility of the Bohemian forest in April 1945 could have been no more different from events that transpired before.

Stewart, the emissary sent to negotiate the surrender of the German Remount Depot on that spring night more than six decades ago, describes his first meeting with the German veterinarian Lessing. Speaking from his home in Amherst, Virginia, Stewart, now eighty-eight, is quick to laugh and easy to listen to, with a light Southern drawl in his voice.

"According to the information that I have, Lessing came out of the woods into our lines with a white flag on a stick and was picked up and taken to Colonel Reed," explains Stewart. "I was in the field at the time and got a message rather late in the day that Colonel Reed wanted to see me at his headquarters. When I got there, I met Lessing, who of course had come through because he'd heard of Colonel Reed."

He could have refused the mission, Stewart acknowledges. Reed later informed him that Patton had said, "If you get in trouble, you are on your own." Given the fact the Allies had allocated Czechoslovakia to the Russians in the Yalta Agreement, there were strict orders not to cross the border. However, there was really no time for deliberation, notes Stewart. The Russians themselves were enroute to Hostau and the fate of the Lipizzaners appeared dim if the Americans were unable to arrive first. (Some thought they would be slaughtered for food.)

Lessing had ridden his Thoroughbred stallion from Hostau, accompanied by a groom leading a Lipizzaner. Near the edge of the woods, the horses were left at the home of a forester, whose motorcycle Lessing borrowed to reach the point where the 2nd Cavalry spotted him.

Stewart describes the return. "When I went back with Lessing, we picked up the motorcycle—he'd stashed it somewhere—I got on behind him and we rode down to the forester's house. That's where we got the horses." An equestrian since youth, Stewart was given the Lipizzaner to ride. "He was a Yugoslavian Lipizzaner, reputed to have been King Peter's favorite mount. He was the easiest and best-mounted horse I ever rode in my life."

It was around two in the morning when Lessing and Stewart reached Hostau, eighteen miles across the border. They promptly headed to the veterinarian's apartment. "Before making the trip, Lessing and another veterinarian, Dr. Wolfgang Kroll, had talked with the colonel in command of the Remount station about surrendering so that they could get the horses safely back to either Germany or Austria and not let them fall into the hands of the Russians," says Stewart. "He apparently changed his mind after Lessing left; he was a Czech national and just learned the Russians would control his country. He told Kroll that if they brought an American in, he would have the three of us shot as spies."

Consequently, Stewart was immediately hidden at Lessing's residence. "He didn't even want his wife to know I was there because Kroll had told her about what this colonel had said about shooting us. Lessing brought me a cup of coffee and we made plans that if we couldn't get to Schultze, we'd try to find the best way for our people to come in from the 2nd Cavalry. As it turned out, we were able to get through to General Schultze."

Recollecting the events of that night, Stewart surmises, "I probably slept, I don't remember now. It seems like I went several days without eating and just lived on coffee."

By ten o'clock the next morning, Lessing, Kroll, and Stewart were horseback searching for an officer who might take them to General Schultze. "We rode around and came to a command post. Lessing explained the mission and what we wanted to accomplish." The three men were soon enroute to see the German General. Stewart recalls an official-looking document fabricated by a quick-thinking regimental staff officer at the 2nd Cavalry prior to his departure, which proved invaluable on the mission. "Major Rollin Steinmetz cut a page from the front of a book for use in naming me as a plenipotentiary to the commanding general from General Patton and Colonel Reed. Patton never knew of the liberty we took."

Yet, Stewart's presence raised concerns. "Schultze questioned my being allowed to view the defenses. They talked about it in German, whether to let me go back or not, I'd seen so much." Had Stewart considered himself a prisoner of war? The genteel Southerner just laughs, "Well, you might say 'sort of.' I wasn't being held prisoner, I was hiding out for awhile."

Instructed before the mission to avoid disclosing the fact that he spoke some German, Stewart quietly noted various conversations in process during the meeting. "One of the colonels on General Schultze's staff said that Adolf (Hitler) had promised them a secret weapon. Some others said, 'Oh, Adolf is kaput.' They said he was finished and most of them seemed to agree. They knew it was over, I'm sure, and the sooner the better," describes Stewart.

"So General Schultze looked at me and in very good English said, 'How many panzers (tanks) can you bring?' That's when I told him that we were aware that his reputation could be at stake and that we didn't want to do anything to jeopardize his standing in the Army, or our interest in saving these horses from falling into the hands of the Russians. I just said, 'You name the number, we are flexible, we can bring any number,'" remarks Stewart. "He looked at me a long time and then pulled out that little note pad and wrote my safe conduct pass [to return]."

Subsequently, the General left with some staff members. Two colonels returned later with a message. "They told us that there would be no defense of the Remount Depot. They didn't say whether we'd have to fight to get there or not, just that no defense would be made on it, which we took to mean that we would be allowed to come in without any problem."

Holz spent a total of twenty-one years in the service and left the Cavalry as a Major. In the years since, he has spoken and written about Operation Cowboy frequently. "Tom Stewart was released in the company of a German veterinarian [Kroll], returned across the front lines to us and put the surrender negotiations into effect. It wasn't very long thereafter, everything was arranged, and we went in and affected the surrender," says Holz, who lives in the midst of Pennsylvania horse country today.

"I was with a line troop," he continues, explaining the progression of events. "Two reconnaissance troops went and they were to extricate the horses and the prisoner of war camp. Other forces, not involved with the rescue and evacuation, went in as protection forces and that was my role."

He explains the surprise that waited. "We were prepared for whatever would happen, but nothing happened. We were met at the gate with an honor guard of German soldiers who saluted us as we drove in between their ranks! We were generally and harmlessly welcomed and from there on it was our show all the way."

A Strange Alliance

In 2001, the Austrian Ambassador in Washington presented Tom Stewart with the Austrian National Gold Award for Services to Agriculture and Forestry for his efforts in rescuing the Lipizzaners. The Tennessee-born veteran relives the massive operation.

"We stayed at Hostau about a week and then moved the horses from Czechoslovakia."

Yet while evacuating the Lipizzaners from the threat of approaching Russian military, a band of "White Russians" (who were also Ukranians), played a crucial role. "They were marvelous horsemen and through their experience we drove the horses overland—the stallions in front and the broodmares behind," explains Stewart. The leader, an avowed anti-communist who went by the single name Amazov, had been returned from exile in Siberia because of his extraordinary talents with horses. "He was probably the best horseman in the world at the time," reflects Stewart.

During Operation Cowboy, 400-plus horses were moved cross-country, including 200 head of Lipizzaners from Austria and another fifty of the rare breed from the Yugoslovian Stud Farm in Bosnia.

"The stallions were up front away from the mares and colts," notes Stewart. "They were not the ones that were performing in the Spanish Riding School at that time. They were the breeding stallions, who had been retired from the school."

The balance of horses included assorted breeds, such as Thoroughbreds, East Prussian horses, and Arabians—including two famous sires Witek and Lotnik.

In less than two full days, the entire herd arrived at a Remount Depot in Germany.

"We didn't stop and take any breaks, we moved right along," recalls Stewart, who rode a portion of the route on the same Lipizzaner stallion he jumped the abatis with. "The only slow down was when we had to stop because of the American tanks crossing our path and trying to take our road."

Even now, Stewart appreciatively notes, "I was amazed at how well it went. Of course, there were quite a few grooms, most of them Polish, and Amazov had about twenty-five men with him, plus his wife and daughter, who were excellent horsewomen. I forget how many American soldiers were involved, I believe about six."

Ironically, Stewart recounts, "I don't think there was a single cowboy in the movement, maybe one Texan. I don't know how it got that name." The euphemism was apparently adopted more after the fact, than during.

Holz reflects on Reed's role in instigating the historic undertaking (which in truth Patton essentially was uninvolved with, according to those who were there). "I think it was a stroke of good luck that the U.S. Army had a distinguished Cavalry commander, who himself was an excellent horseman. He recognized that anything left behind would become Russian." Holz's comments reveal great admiration for his long-ago superior. "I visited him several times in Virginia and every morning, he went out and rode his horse and then came back to breakfast."

"He was a no-nonsense guy. That doesn't mean he was a stick in the mud, but when there was a job to do you did it. When there was no job to do and you felt like partying, then fine, no harm done. But duty came first and a high quality of effort was always demanded. He died at age seventy-nine in 1980 and we were all shocked. Forever and ever since we knew him, he was regarded as indestructible and here he died. How mortal can one get? That's how people regarded Charles Reed," Holz remembers.

The gong of a clock sounds in the background at Stewart's home as he mentions the Sunday school lesson he is preparing to teach in two days on grace and faith. For the moment, it's more on his mind than horses.

After completing his military service in 1946, Stewart spent thirty years with the Tennessee Department of Revenue, eighteen of which he was Director of the Motor Vehicle Division. From 1947 until 1990 he bred pleasure horses on a limited scale, using Tennessee Walking, Arabian, and Morgan bloodlines. "Just as many as I could afford," laughs Stewart. He considers what they have added to his life. "If you knew a horse, you could depend on him and if he was going to do something bad, you could depend on him to do that too. I always understood horses better than I did people."

Meanwhile, in his postmilitary years, Holz found greater satisfaction as a writer, the "wr" kind he notes, than as a rider. He reflects, "I think animals, in general, give a positive perspective to people around the world. Unless you learn to understand, appreciate, and love animals, you have that much less understanding and appreciation and love for humans. To that extent I think that horses, to a larger extent, are just a piece of the puzzle."

Bridge Between Cultures

In twenty years of diplomatic service, Peter Launsky-Tieffenthal was stationed in Washington, D.C., Saudi Arabia, and twice in India, before beginning his current five-year tenure in Los Angeles as the Consul General of Austria. Born in Vienna, Launsky-Tieffenthal recalls the omnipresent feature of the Spanish Riding School and its famous white stallions. Located near Vienna's Imperial Palace, it was walking distance from the university he attended. "It's one of the reasons why people approach us about Austria—they want to know what they need to do to visit and watch the stallions in action," he explains.

Launsky-Tieffenthal grew up riding, almost daily for twenty-five years. Before beginning his diplomatic career, he competed in three-day eventing, reveling in the multiple challenges of cross-country jumping, stadium jumping, and dressage. His accomplished equestrian skills have proved a boon in bridging cultures and furthering understanding in diverse ways.

"In all the countries that I've lived in, plus others that I've visited on horseback, that's the experience I've had," remarks Launsky-Tieffenthal. "For example, we went through the plains of Hungary without understanding the local language. The horse was a means of establishing bridges to the local population, who cherish horses. One felt welcome at all times, at all places. The same was true for India. During my first couple of months there, I was unable to communicate with many people other than through sharing the experience of horseback riding," describes the dark-haired statesman.

In his travels from country to country, Launsky-Tieffenthal has observed differing perspectives on humans and horses. "There are countries where the individual is trying to impose himself on the horse, create a partnership with a subordinate, human being over the horse," he describes. "And other cultures where that partnership seems more on par, kind of two equal partners. In most cases, over longer periods of time, that proves to be the much more successful one and I gather, also much more pleasant for both."

Yet, beyond a bridge between cultures, Launsky-Tieffenthal believes the horse offers a bridge between human beings and nature. "I think it allows you to experience nature differently than say, walking or biking. When you ride through the forests of Austria, there's a good chance you may pass by deer and stag and fox at very close range because wildlife feels not intimated by other creatures, by other animals. Whereas, if you were to walk, they would sort of disappear and vanish in advance of your getting to a particular spot. That is something that I experienced as I grew up. Maybe it is also a reflection," ponders the Consul General. "The way people treat their horses and how they behave in nature with a horse very often proves to be a very accurate reflection of their character in day-to-day life. Their temperament, their discipline, the depth of their feelings. In that sense also, it's something that's been very educational," Launsky-Tieffenthal reflects.

Historic Link

"If you walk through the streets of Vienna, there are many, many monuments that show former emperors and members of the Imperial family on horseback on all sorts of occasions. I think they are kind of a constant reminder of the significance that horses have played historically in Austria. The Lipizzaners and the Spanish Riding School are kind of a continuation of that legacy," he notes. "It's a centerpiece for both Austrians and foreigners, when they spend time in Vienna."

If one thinks interest has waned in displays of the art of classical equitation which has flourished at the Spanish Riding School for more than 400 years, try getting tickets to the Sunday performances in the Baroque riding hall with less than a two- or three-year wait. "The Sunday performances still need a lot of lead time," Launsky-Tieffenthal admits. "However, the weekly morning workouts and practice sessions are quite easily accessible. Most people say, 'I'd rather go for those sessions and not miss watching the Lipizzaners.'"

Whatever the case, spectators will witness a living tribute to the efforts of the 2nd Cavalry and how two different sides of a political fence successfully worked together because of horses.

The E-ssential Barometer

There is an unmistakable trace of wistfulness in Launsky-Tieffenthal's voice as he describes how often he currently rides. "Unfortunately, far too little," he admits. The absence has only made more clear, all that it represents. "I think horse riding is a meditative experience, as much as it is a spiritual one. Because of its sensitivities, the horse is kind of a barometer. You cannot hide your own emotions in front of a horse, so the horse kind of forces you to be honest, not only with the horse, but with yourself. If you try to do that and let go, then it becomes like meditation in nature, jointly with another beast," reflects Launsky-Tieffenthal. "I think that's something I probably only realized well into my riding and some of it, only retrospectively, because I notice the kind of healing effect that it had on both body and mind."

☊ Try This

Organize a lunch or dinner with a group of horse friends (or aspiring ones). For those who thrive on theme parties, here's your chance. Create your own equine embassy with "official state dinner" invitations. Make it a potluck, or cook to your heart's content. For table favors, provide pen or pencil and five index cards for each guest. Have an empty wicker basket available. Ask each guest to write down five examples—one per card—that answer the following question. How do horses help me collaborate with other human beings? (In other words, how do horses help me to bridge differences with other people?) When finished, fold the cards in half and drop in basket. Names are not required. Remove basket from table and mix well. Before dessert, pass the basket around the table and ask each guest to draw a card for five successive rounds until all the cards are drawn (each guest should have five). Beginning with the host/hostess, stand up and read one card per round (no peeking inside before reading), which will obviously proceed five times around the table. Conclude the process with thanks for the guests' participation, offer a final toast to "the noble horse," and proceed without further delay to dessert. In addition to providing a catalyst for discussions that may last well into the night, this can also raise consciousness about ways the horse is relevant today.

Should you experience sudden wanderlust, check out Austria travel information and the Spanish Riding School of Vienna on the Internet at *www.austria-tourism.at* or head directly to the School at *www.spanische-reitschule.com*. Currently, there are only about 3,000 purebred Lipizzaners in the world; more than half of that total are now located in the United States. For more information see the United States Lipizzan Registry at *www.lipizzan-uslr.com*.

Chapter Thirteen

Freedom
. . . the leap of a lifetime

*In the end, the question is, am
I myself? If you are not yourself,
you are not free . . .*
—Ihaleakala Hew Len, Ph.D.

EACH MORNING AS JEANNE ROSENBERG
leaves the house to go to work, she looks out
across the tree-dotted acreage of her Topanga Canyon home in
Southern California. Heading up a well-traveled path to a rustic
barn on the hill, she climbs a flight of stairs to an office on the
second floor of the stable where four of her reining horses live.
Sitting down at the computer amidst an ambiance of animals and

outdoors, the words to a new Hollywood screenplay emerge as Rosenberg begins the day's countdown until she gets to ride.

Reining in Opportunity

"I wanted to be anything but a writer in film school. I absolutely knew that was nothing I would ever be doing," says Rosenberg, who inadvertently launched a screenwriting career straight out of graduate school, after sending director Carroll Ballard an unsolicited script analysis of Walter Farley's first novel, *The Black Stallion*. "It was a required class, Script Analysis, and there was an assignment to read something." Rosenberg reread her favorite childhood book, the Farley classic, and "fell in love with it again." As fate would have it, the timing couldn't have been better. Shortly after completing graduate school at USC School of Cinema-Television in Los Angeles (often called USC Film School), Rosenberg learned that producer Francis Ford Coppola and Ballard—a director she much admired—were turning Farley's book into a film.

"I loved Carroll Ballard's short films. They were absolutely brilliant!" recalls Rosenberg. "Any rate, I sent a letter to Carroll and subsequently got a phone call from him saying, 'I really like what you wrote. We'll have to get together.' Time passes, we don't get together. I call the production office, they say, 'Oh, they're already in Canada in preproduction.' I call them in Canada. 'Do you mind if I drop in?'" she continues describing, in the tempo of an accomplished storyteller. The clock turns back to 1977 as

Rosenberg relates a course of action that has shaped her life ever since.

"This man I've never met is now back-pedaling, I can see it through the phone. I can see him going, 'Oh no!' but he said, 'OK.' So I fly to Canada on my way to Peoria (Illinois) to visit the family. It was kind of on the way. I spent about three days there and I was in heaven. They were all absolutely crazed; they were about to shoot the film. There had been several scripts through the years, but he won't decide on any of them. He has an actress that no part has ever been written for. They're a little nuts and we meet for breakfast one morning. He was late and I'm doo-dling some notes on a napkin." Rosenberg laughs, remembering how Ballard grabbed the napkin in the frenzy of the moment.

Soon after arriving home, Rosenberg got a phone call to come work on the movie. Partnered with screenwriter Melissa Mathison (who later wrote *ET*), the two adapted Farley's book into the screenplay *The Black Stallion*, starring Kelly Reno, Mickey Rooney, and Teri Garr.

"We started shooting 7-7-77," says Rosenberg, citing a date numerologists would find significant. "It was everybody's first feature—Carroll Ballard, Melissa (Mathison), Daleb Deschanel, the cinematographer." For Rosenberg, the experience was not only a first, but as extraordinary as anything imaginable in her horse-crazed youth, right down to meeting author Walter Farley, an idol. "He had been like God when I was growing up. I never even imagined that there was a person to go with that name. I could barely talk," says Rosenberg, doing a good imitation of a breathless fan while candidly describing herself. "It was all very thrilling."

Hard-Wired for Horses

The popular movie, released in 1979, not only established an unanticipated career path for Rosenberg, but did so with the zeal of a childhood passion unleashed. "As a little kid, I was obsessed with horses. It's a common language. You've all read the same books, have all the little plastic horses, you're galloping around the school yard. Today's kids are still doing the same things," says Rosenberg, adding, "I guess some of the books are different."

Born and raised in the heartland of America, Rosenberg was first exposed to horses when her older sister, Joni, got interested. While the primary focus of the local equestrian community revolved around Quarter Horses and trail riding, Rosenberg and her sister wound up at a barn with a Saddlebred trainer, who abruptly moved soon after the girls' father bought them a gigantic Saddlebred named Masterpiece. Standing 17½ hands tall (seventy inches at the withers), the horse fortunately lived up to his name. "I was a pretty little kid and I just walked underneath this horse's belly standing straight up. He was a great horse," she recalls. "My sister dropped out (of horses) and I just stuck with it."

Like a switch that stays on once activated, Rosenberg's passion for horses took flight as if on automatic pilot and has remained ever-present. "It's absolutely genetic. I know it is. It's hard-wired," smiles the screenwriter. "You can't help it if you're a kid and you couldn't help it if you're a parent. You can't give your kid this and you can't take it away. It's just either there or not," continues Rosenberg, whose daughter, Erica Rose, got the career gene and launched a fashion designer career straight out of Brown University after taking her handmade clothes to several trendy retailers. "I don't want to get loony, but kids come out with different gifts and different talents. Your ability to bond with animals, work with animals, or particular animals, that's in there too."

Writer's Reward

As Rosenberg segued from *The Black Stallion* to firmly establish her name in Hollywood, her rapport with horses and animals, at large, have helped promote an accomplished film career—sometimes in roundabout ways. Her original screenplay *The Journey of Natty Gann*, produced by Disney, saw Rosenberg also credited as associate producer, in a tale where a wolf played a supporting part. For another Disney movie, *White Fang*, with a wolf a key character, she worked with producer Mike Lobell to adapt Jack London's novel for the screen. For Jean Jacques Annaud's film *Running Free*, Rosenberg returned undaunted from a near-harrowing research trip to Namibia, to write a screenplay originally inspired by a real-life wild horse band in the African desert. (*Running Free* released in a drastically altered form, was far from the original vision, although the equine performers are excellent.)

More recently, Rosenberg has penned a string of screenplays for IMAX productions such as *China: The Panda Adventure*, *T-Rex: Back to the Cretaceous*, and *The Young Black Stallion*, released in 2003, which she also executive produced, a symbolic full circle for her career. A prequel to the film that launched Rosenberg into Hollywood, the IMAX movie was based on the novel *The Young Black Stallion*, written by Walter Farley and his son Steven Farley.

Still, the unsung heroes of all Rosenberg's screenplays are the writer's very own horses. A constant presence most of her life, they remain a powerful daily incentive.

"Riding is my reward. I have to go to work first and write my five pages each day," explains Rosenberg. If she finishes early, it's all the more time to ride.

"As you sit there, you're getting more and more tense. Then I ride and it just evaporates. I like the physical work of dealing with the horse," says Rosenberg. "Showing is another great release. It's so divorced from my 'real world.' It's like a vacation—it takes me to a whole other sea of people. You're connected in this way that's really physical."

The owner of six Quarter Horses, Rosenberg competes in reining, a fast-growing sport where horses perform spins, circles, and sliding stops at the slightest cue from the rider. "If you ask for a lead change and your timing is off, the horse is going to bobble and you're going to get penalized for it," she notes. "One of the things my trainer says is, 'Make your point and then move on.' It's the pressure and the release. You've made your point and now you move on." In other words, the secret is akin to riding the yin and yang.

Rosenberg wraps up her fifth and final page for the day, quickly transforming from writer to rider. For a moment, she considers the long-running impact of her first movie; twenty-five years after its original release, *The Black Stallion* is now on DVD. "People generally have been moved by the film. I think Carroll Ballard's a very special and unique filmmaker," reflects Rosenberg. "Onscreen, you see this man loves horses and loves that spirit and wildness and energy. He really captured all of those qualities and something else. The bond that forms between the boy and the horse is so incredibly strong. That's the one that we're all searching for—that kind of bond in all of our great relationships."

The Horse Catalyst

Tedi Tate zips up her black leather jacket, shoves a mane of hair inside a helmet, and climbs aboard her Harley-Davidson Sportster 1200 in riding boots and britches. Throttling down Pacific Coast Highway toward her home in Venice, Tate shifts gears on the motorcycle she rode home from Montana to California after finishing production on *The Horse Whisperer*, a lifetime ago in many ways.

"My marriage was breaking up on that film and my life was changing. I was in Montana six months on location, a place I'd always wanted to go," remembers Tate, who was tapped to work as assistant prop master on the movie, partly because of her background in horses.

Born in Fort Worth, Texas, immersed in the hub of Lone Star horse culture, Tate first climbed into the saddle at "two or three" and became immediately obsessed. "I have pictures of me on this old pinto mare named Dolly," she fondly recalls. The passion continued, basically unimpeded, until Tate set course on a film industry career in her twenties and a seesaw of callings commenced.

"I would start riding again and then I would be swept away by the schedule of a film," remarks Tate, a petite five-foot-two, who is quick to smile. "Like any of the physical disciplines, if you don't stay with it regularly, you can't really progress, so it was very frustrating. I'd get in it and I'd get out, but I would always get back again with horses. It was just an irresistible draw."

Little could Tate have anticipated how working on *The Horse Whisperer* would accelerate the impending crossroad in her career and magnify the personal priorities that it did.

"I was working with these fantastic horse people. Buck Brannaman was almost magical in what he could do with horses," Tate recalls. One of a team of top horsemen on the film, Brannaman worked closely with Robert Redford, the "horse whisperer," to coach the star on the nuances of such real-life practices used with horses. As part of Tate's advance work for the prop department, she was sent to one of Brannaman's horsemanship clinics (which take place throughout the country). "It was a really good way to start researching the entire clinician scene. One horse in particular was really bad," says Tate. "That horse had a bag of tricks like I have never seen and Buck just went through all of them unfazed until the horse kind of came to the end of his repertoire."

Yet on location during *The Horse Whisperer*, the day-to-day realities of film work often put Tate at odds with her equine interests.

"I was surrounded by horses and yet I couldn't really be part of them. I was on the outside and I wanted to be on the inside. I wanted to be with the horses and I couldn't because I had this barrier of working on the movie. I didn't even get to ride," she recalls. "I didn't have time. I was working really hard on the film."

In effect, Tate's motorcycle became a horse substitute. "I was riding it a lot there. When I was in Montana, I seriously considered buying a horse and riding it home to California. It sounds crazy now," Tate laughs. "I really thought of that."

Whimsical or not, an auto accident in Montana dispelled Tate's riding aspirations for a time and acerbated an increasing assortment of physical manifestations from the demands of long-term prop department work.

Tate admitted it was time to make a permanent change, when a recurring shoulder injury came to a head during a television pilot she was working on after *The Horse Whisperer* and forced her into a lengthy rehabilitation. After fifteen years in the business, the change required soul-searching.

Making Sensitivity a Plus

"I was wanting to do something where being sensitive was an asset and not a weakness," explains Tate. "And, the film business is not particularly the place for that, except maybe if you're an actor."

In the course of three operations on her shoulder, Tate had plenty of time for contemplation. "I knew I had to rehab and do something else. I started being really practical. I realized that leaving the film industry meant leaving a job of pretty nice status, with a good salary, even though the overtime was a killer. It had a lot of perks," she describes. "It was interesting, people always liked to talk to me about my work. I traveled a lot, learned so much, met great people, and did fascinating research for my department, all the time. It was hard to leave, but it was totally absorbing. I had no life other than that."

Yet in facing her problems head-on, an unexpected revelation emerged. "I realized that it was going to be really difficult and I would probably have to deal with financial hardship and loss of status. There would be a lot of difficult emotions to go through and hard work. I thought, 'Wait a minute! If I'm going to go through all that anyway, why become some practical thing that I don't really have any passion for? Why not do something I love? Why not really try to follow a dream?'" In doing so, Tate recognized the time had come to embrace a long-ignored desire. "To me, to actually make a living working with animals that you love and people that work with them is a dream." Synchronicity and a canine friend set her hopes in motion.

The Equine Entente

"It's a really funny coincidence. I wanted to ride, but I just didn't have the nerve," says Tate, recollecting the rehab phase that followed her surgeries. "It was raining hard one day and I'd been walking my dog Beau. I brought her in and she was muddy, so I threw down some papers for her to walk on. One of the things was a Santa Monica College schedule of classes. My dog stepped on it, slid, and she opened it to the page on Horsemanship," Tate still marvels. "I didn't even know it was in there. I looked at it and said, 'Wow! I think my shoulders are good enough I could try that.' So I called up the number and registered for it. My dog really helped me out on that one."

Tate not only began riding again, but enrolled in a variety of college courses, including a number of equine science classes at Pierce College in Woodland Hills, which has programs oriented toward careers in the horse industry. "Many people in the horse industry have been in it all their lives. I've kind of had a foot in it and a foot out. I rode and read everything about horses. That does serve me, but it's not the same as having done it for twenty years," she contemplates.

"I'd like to get to the point where I can teach and someday train, but for now, I'm interested in all aspects of it," says Tate, who spent a recent summer as a groom. "To me it is endlessly fascinating to study the history of humans and horses together. It's a really interesting deal that the two species have made. It's a peculiar bargain," observes Tate, who has traveled as far as the Ecole Nationale d'Equitation (French National Riding School) in Saumur, France, to further her riding skills since making the dramatic midlife career leap.

"I firmly believe that horses have a great sense of humor. Some of them are hysterical." Tate has no regrets about the choice she made, only more appreciation as it further progresses. "Horses definitely are teaching me about real patience and kind-ness—the incalculable value of kindness," says Tate. They will repay you a hundred times."

Tate reflects, "What's happening now is a rekindling. I can feel it. I'm on the inside now. I'm not making much money, but I'm working up to something. I'm learning an enormous amount and I'm amongst the horses now. They accept me."

The Might of "My Way"

The earthen scent of Russy Forest, still damp with early morning mist, surrounds seven horses traveling at a fast-paced trot, intent on their destination. Waylaid by fresh-baked croissants and rich French coffee, replenished multiple times, the group rides a healthy chunk of kilometers to reach Château de Chambord for an eleven o'clock equestrian spectacle. Just in time, Anne-France Launay guides her American guests through a side entrance to the UNESCO world heritage site, their mounts already unsaddled and lunching in a nearby field. Breathtakingly beautiful and nearly inconceivable as a sixteenth-century undertaking, Chambord calls across chapters of French history as its 365 chimneys etch the sky.

"The most natural way to visit the Loire Valley Châteaux is on horseback, the way people used to travel throughout the region," remarks Launay, a former advertising executive turned entrepreneur who heeded the call of horses and traded her briefcase for saddle bags. A certified riding instructor and trail guide, Launay christened Cheval & Châteaux (Horse and Châteaux) in 2001, after several years of planning. Offering intimate horseback treks through the Loire Valley, she choreographs accommodations in private châteaux, gourmet picnics, castle tours, and plentiful riding with the attention once devoted to major advertising campaigns—right down to the Cheval & Châteaux–monogrammed saddle pads.

"At thirty-five years old, I started a new life, rich with a lot of new experiences," remarks Launay, who worked in advertising for fourteen years, after starting out as a copywriter for Young & Rubicam in her twenties. She and her husband opened their own company when they got married, her third agency. However, her interest in advertising soon ran its course. "I felt less and less happy in my job and was spending more and more time with my horse. In 1995, I started competing again in show jumping. Business was hard and I decided to stop." Leaving advertising proved to be a life-altering decision.

Raised in the north of France near Lille, an industrial part of the country, Launay describes the area as one "where the climate is hard and the people very warm." By age ten she'd felt the bite of the horse bug, however, it took Launay nearly a year to actually get in the saddle. Thanks to a cousin who started riding, she landed her first opportunity at the same stable. After her first mount, Quereuller (quarreler) proved to be "a horse who didn't want to move at all," Launay experienced the opposite in a group lesson, her second attempt. All of the horses were cantering and she felt herself slipping. "I asked where I could fall because there were not a lot of places," she mentions. Undaunted, Launay notes, "And I never stopped riding until I was twenty-three years old and began working as a copywriter." With lack of time to maintain her level of riding while working, she left the sport for seven years.

The tables turned when she bought her first horse at thirty, putting advertising on the exit route from her life. Launay first made the leap as a riding instructor, which requires examinations, and licensing in France. Then came a fortuitous meeting with some visiting Germans who wanted to ride around the area's châteaux, which were virtually in her backyard.

Launay comments, "The idea of doing something with horses and châteaux was born on that day. I decided to realize this project and created Cheval & Châteaux. I did it exactly the way I wanted."

The True Life

Launay may have left the advertising business, but her copywriting skills are still evident in her brochure. "You will enjoy the magic of old stone dwellings, of hundred-year-old trees, and of the Lord's authentic and cordial welcome," it reads. And what the brochure promises, she delivers. The rapport Launay achieves with her guests clearly exudes the joy that passion plus profession can yield.

"I love the first morning of the treks when the van arrives with the horses. Often it is still cold," says Launay, who organizes rides from May through October. "I love the first morning when we stop talking about the horses and we are with the horses. In one second, the context changes totally." For several days, a group experiences the past and present at once, in the sort of time warp possible aboard horses. "There is a magic moment when we arrive at each château on horseback, as it slowly becomes bigger and bigger with the rhythm of the horse's walk," Launay relates.

She's never had any second thoughts about the choice to leave advertising for an existence where horses, people, weather, and unplanned events take a new twist every day—and she doesn't expect to.

"Working with horses is hard physically, especially in winter," admits Launay, who teaches riding in the off-season. "You don't make a lot of money and there are not a lot of holidays, or weekends, but it's a true life." Plus there's a show jumper named Hidalgo, Launay's eight-year-old sport horse. "Horseback riding keeps me in life everyday," she reflects. "It makes me have true relations with others and with nature."

Pure Heart

"Freedom is about being yourself," says Ihaleakala Hew Len, Ph.D., an educator and practitioner of the ancient Hawaiian problem-solving practice Ho'oponopono. "The memories that live in our subconscious are incredible. When they play they pre-empt our identities," continues Hew Len, who trained with the late Kahuna Lapa'au Morrnah Nalamaku Simeona. For more than two decades Hew Len has traveled the world lecturing and teaching the Ho'oponopono process, including two presentations at the United Nations. Simeona, his mentor, was designated a Living Treasure of Hawaii in 1983, and updated Ho'oponopono for modern use.

"Being yourself means not having all these other programs going that dictate how you should spend your life," remarks Hew Len, in between bites of a sandwich. "You think everything is 'out there,' but it's not. It's you," he insists. "To know a horse, you have to know yourself."

In the eighties, Hew Len worked as a staff psychologist for the criminally insane at Hawaii State Hospital. Before that, he was Executive Director for the Hawaii Association for Retarded Citizens and an educator.

"If I were going to train a horse, I would do it the same way I would train a child," remarks Hew Len. "The way is to come first with a pure heart. You've got to come empty. Nothing going on. No judgment. If you come with a pure heart, the horse will learn effortlessly because you're going to tune right into the horse's rhythm and the horse will show you what it is that it can do."

Born in Hawaii, Hew Len splits his time between the Islands and Los Angeles. Quick-witted and unwavering in his commitment to the Ho'oponopono process—erasing errors in thinking based on past memories—Hew Len sidesteps a mention that he's featured in the Timothy Freke book, *Shamanistic Wisdomkeepers: Shamanism in the Modern World.*

"So how do you come with a pure heart? You have to be free," he continues. "Allowing your rhythm and the horse just to weave something so beautiful you just go 'wow.' And he, the horse, can get a sense of it. Instead of you just riding the horse, it's you riding the horse, who's riding the land—that connection," adds Hew Len, digging into a bowl of strawberries and grapes.

"The intellect was not created to know. It was created to choose. The basic choice is to be or not to be your identity as first created by the Divinity in his image," explains Hew Len. "Freedom is being able to be open so you will hear, what is right and perfect for that being and that being will respond." Hew Len reflects, "At the end, the question for anything is, 'Am I myself?' I cannot experience a horse otherwise."

☊ TRY THIS

For the fearless—find an empty horse stall and set up camp for an hour. Wear a watch or bring an alarm and close the door once inside. You will also need a trash bag and several carrots. Take along five magazines, not to read, but to tear apart. Randomly open the magazines four or five times apiece, ripping out one page each time. When finished, inspect the pages and place them in order of your preference from most to least appealing. Five minutes before your hour is up, starting with the favorite, crumple each page quickly, toss it in the garbage bag, and immediately proceed to the next. When time's up, take your belongings, exit, and dump the bag in the trash. As for the carrots, leave all but one behind for the stall's real-life equine occupant. The final carrot is for you. Consider whether you simply sat in a horse stall for an hour, or performed a symbolic act of freedom in the process.

Freedom opens the door to options—all manners of things previously unrecognized. According to the American Horse Council (AHC), the United States horse industry makes a $112.1 billion total impact on the nation's gross domestic product. Yet the figure is far from common knowledge. Likewise, opportunities exist, virtually around the globe, for livelihoods in the horse world. The AHC's annual horse industry directory offers a comprehensive and economical reference guide, including rodeo organizations to equine libraries and museums, plus state horse councils to breed associations. Find out more at *www.horsecouncil.org*.

If you're itching to get a quick international overview, visit *www.equistaff.com*, an equine employment site, which lists jobs by countries, states, breeds, and employment type. Resumes are accepted, too.

For others, the literal call of the unknown represents ultimate freedom. Traveling abroad and riding to castles where you hitch your mount to a tree before sightseeing offers an experience unlike any tour bus. Get a glimpse at *www.cheval-et-chateaux.com*.

For an overview of Ho'oponopono, the ancient Hawaiian problem-solving practice, see *www.hooponopono.org*.

Chapter Fourteen

Creativity
. . . inspiration unbridled

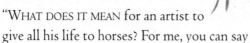

*Art is the intention you give to
something. If there is no intention,
it's just movement. The difference is
demonstration and art . . .*
—Bartabas

"WHAT DOES IT MEAN for an artist to
give all his life to horses? For me, you can say
that the horse is the instinct and the man is the intellect. So it helps
you understand," says Bartabas, the wiry, intense founder of Théâter
Zingaro, the extolled performing troupe of horses and humans.
"The more people know, the less they feel. Unless we are able to feel,
in a way, we are less intelligent than the horse or animals in general."

Mystical Marriage

The Paris Metro rumbles beneath the surface of the City of
Light, bound in the direction of La Courneuve. As the subway

Line 7 clatters to a halt at the Fort d'Aubervilliers stop, doors spring open, and an American passenger disembarks looking for the now-familiar "sortie" signs indicating the exit. Stepping into daylight at the top of a narrow escalator, directions are needed no more. The prominent entrance to the French equestrian theatre troupe's home base is steps away and the yellow-painted name *Zingaro* jumps from red and green gypsy caravans in the distance like echoes to the sign overhead.

In several hours, the buzz of 1,300 spectators will fill a lofty wooden structure in the forefront, as a mélange of Parisians and tourists await the ritualistic start of the evening performance. Then, at the designated moment, the crowd will pour across the grounds, released like a stream of humanity, and funnel up two stairways into a stable in the distance. Two second-floor walkways—over stalls of blanketed horses, past hanging chandeliers—will lead them to the entrances of an incense-infused theater. As the hour for Zingaro's "Loungta, Les Chevaux De Vent" (Loungta, The Horses of Wind) approaches, few can fathom the spiritual impact of chanting Tibetan monks, horses, dancers, and equestrian performers. Yet, if audiences from Moscow to Amsterdam are indicative, spectators will leave with a sense of quiet, full of some inner nectar, easier observed than described. Before the theater empties, Bartabas, Zingaro's one-name creative genius, will already be back in the stable, devoid of makeup from four appearances in the show.

"For twenty years now, I'm speaking about the same things, the relation between man and horse. For each performance it's a different pretext," says the internationally acclaimed director, choreographer, and horseman who founded Zingaro in 1984. The troupe, some forty people total, live on site with the horses when not touring.

Timeless at forty-six, with short-cropped dark hair and near boot-shaped sideburns, Bartabas journeyed to the Gyuto Monastery in northeast India, a refuge of exiled Tibetan monks, one-and-a-half years before "Loungta" debuted to recruit ten monks—age twenty to seventy. The eighth production Bartabas has created portraying the mystical relationship between man and horse, "Loungta" exudes sights, rituals, and sounds of Tibet's unique civilization and spirituality, marrying the comparative whisper of hoofbeats with the encompassing "buffalo voices" of the Gyoto monks in maroon robes.

Authentic Self

"My objective is not to do a performance and have people say, 'Look, they ride very well or the music is good.' Of course we ride well. That's our job. The objective of the performance is to make emotion," remarks Bartabas. "That's why I tell the people in the company, 'You have to come inside of the horse when you are working, to hear your horse during the performance. You are not there to smile at the public. We at Zingaro are not playing a role, we are playing ourselves.'" He adds, "I'm not Bartabas one hour in the evening during the performance and somebody else during the day."

Born and raised in France, Bartabas started two theater companies before Zingaro, his first at seventeen. Zingaro represented the merger of a childhood passion with the arts. "My parents were not in the horse business. The only thing they told me is when I was very small I started looking at the horses along the road and I was fascinated," mentions Bartabas. "I always say, it's a passion you cannot explain. I do not know or even want to know why."

A compelling presence in the actual productions, Bartabas has been seen cantering horses backward, engaged in a tête-a-tête with a sitting horse, and performing movements such as a piaffe (trot in place) to the peal of bell chimes. His four appearances as a lone rider in "Loungta" punctuate a theatrical experience where twenty-eight horses take on the roles of animal guides in a Tibetan-inspired production with vaulters, bareback riders, and scenes with whirling equestrians in ceremonial masks.

Living an Art

Bartabas muses, "I am always fascinated by the faces of musicians while they are playing. If you see a violinist or a pianist, sometimes the face is very strange. They are so into their music, they don't know how they appear. This is the way I believe you have to concentrate to get inside your horse."

Sipping tea inside a brightly-colored caravan, smoke curls from his cigarette. "We have a very original way of working. We live at the place where we work," describes Bartabas. "First, we need to be near the horses day and night. It's like children. The second reason is to really live your art." An indoor riding arena, dance studio, and multiple stabling areas are intermixed with trees, caravans, and administration offices on the acreage Zingaro calls home. "There are forty people so it's very important, each one lives in his own area, makes his own food, has his own life," says Bartabas, who is married and has two sons. "The theater must be the human adventure. If the everyday life is not interesting, the performance cannot be interesting."

As such, the delicate and curious thread of the troupe's intertwined lives, separate-yet-together, plays out in extraordinary ways, which Zingaro's first West Coast engagement in 2002 succinctly demonstrated. Taking advantage of a day off during the California run, two separate carloads of performers hit the highway to see Las Vegas as soon as the horses were bedded down after a Wednesday night show. One group, however, drove to Las Vegas, unbelievably, via a route that first took in the Grand Canyon. Although a tentative rendezvous on the Strip had been planned before both cars departed, the time had long come and gone when troupe members from both sightseeing expeditions crossed paths in a Las Vegas casino. A literal manifestation of the art they live, the encounter typified the kind of things Zingaro members experience.

Dauntless Desire

"I always say the perfect horse doesn't exist. I meet horses like I meet people—when you see somebody and fall in love. I find a horse and I like him. I don't know why sometimes, it can be the way they move, sometimes it can be just the look, sometimes it can be the color," explains Bartabas, who brought a herd of palominos from South America for "Loungta" months before the production began.

"People are the same. I learned that through the horse. For me, the definition of talent is the desire," comments Bartabas. "That's why, when I choose somebody for the company, or the horse, I always choose the people that have the most desire. Of course, they have to have the technical motions, but when you have the desire to give something, it's more important. The technical you can learn."

The world-famous artist, who schools the horses he actually performs on, typically begins each day in the saddle. "The composition of the man on the horse is a total thing. It is not the man doing something and the horse doing something," Bartabas explains. "The horse is like a mirror. He'll give you your image. When something goes wrong with the horse, it's always your fault. You have to ask, 'Why did the horse make a mistake, because I explained badly or there's something I didn't do right?'"

Straightforward, Bartabas moves on to another topic, "The horse has taught me a lot because they teach you to live with instinct." He explains, "My definition of instinct is the right movement at the right moment. It's served me in all my life—in the way I am, the way I manage the company even. I always do it by instinct; there's no calculation."

Artistic Evolution

Among the most popular theater tickets in Europe, Zingaro is known around the world in performing arts and equestrian circles alike. While the troupe has traveled to the United States three times and toured numerous countries, Bartabas is steadfast in keeping Zingaro true to its origins. "I never do a performance because somebody asks me to do it. I create a performance when I think inside I'm ready to do it, because inside we have something different to say. Not because the last show was good or not good."

In marked contrast to Hollywood movie sequels, Zingaro's rapport with audiences resembles a dynamic dialogue. "People know that when Zingaro does a new performance, each time it's an event. It's not something we do very quickly. I take my time, one performance every two or three years," says Bartabas, who religiously includes many long-time tour stops on the schedule for each new production.

Bartabas explains, "I prefer to have a long relationship with a town. For me, that's the adventure of theater. You meet every two or three years during life. It's not just one performance. It's an evolution."

Evolution, however, can yield landmark surprises. In February 2003, a new chapter in Bartabas's equestrian artistry took place when Académie du Spectacle Equestre (Academy of Equestrian Spectacles), which he founded and directs, opened in the Grande Ecurie (Grand Stable) at Château de Versailles. Created to perpetuate the equestrian and artistic accomplishments which have earned Zingaro acclaim, the Academy offers a two-year program with training in diverse equestrian pursuits, along with a curriculum that includes drawing, sculpture, music, dance, martial arts, and fencing, among others. According to plan, students from around the world selected for the first class were primarily women—a point Bartabas believes will be preferable for the public and a distinguishing element from the traditionally male-dominated Spanish Riding School in Vienna and France's Cadre Noir in Saumur.

Featuring rare blue-eyed Portuguese horses with cream-colored coats (reputedly the favored breed of Louis XIV), most of the equine contingent came directly to the Academy after touring with Zingaro for three years on "Triptyk," the show preceding "Loungta."

A rare opportunity for the public to see the making of equestrian spectacles, the Academy's morning training sessions can be viewed from a spectator deck in the Grand Stable every day the Château itself is open.

"For me the theater is something sacred," comments Bartabas, who is choreographing full-fledged spectacles at the Academy in addition to his ever-central presence in Zingaro.

"Of course there is spirituality in what we are doing. There's an obligation when you are working in art," he remarks. "For me, spirituality is a way to balance the physical and the inspiration to make something." Standing up, Bartabas stretches, then leaves to climb on a horse.

Allure of Horses

For a man who never requires riding boots, Normand Latourelle is nonetheless acutely aware that forty bales of hay a day are among the essential logistics for the success of his newest multi-media production, "Cavalia: An Equestrian Fantasy." An equestrian extravaganza on tour in North America with the continent's largest traveling big top, "Cavalia" represents a milestone for Latourelle, President and Artistic Director of Voltige, Inc., the Canadian-based company producing the show.

The visionary behind many varied and memorable shows, Latourelle helped build Cirque du Soleil, serving as Vice-President and General Manager from 1985 to 1990. Known for innovative and adventurous productions, his credits include the likes of the City of Montréal's 350th anniversary celebration, "Légendes Fantastiques" (a large-scale multimedia summertime show in Québec), and the 2001 Summit of the Americas in Québec City.

"When I first started to work with Cirque du Soleil, I didn't know anything about horses," recalls Latourelle. "What impressed me is the aesthetic. They have such beautiful bodies, like the aesthetic of an acrobat. When I see them run and react, they are very dynamic. It reminds me of an acrobat doing tumbling or working on the trapeze. Of course, one has two legs and the other has four legs," adds Latourelle in an amiable tone.

A confirmed nonequestrian, Latourelle laughs, "No, I never ride! Neither do I do trapeze, even though I've worked with acrobats for fifteen years. I don't go on the trapeze and don't go on horses."

Exploring man's timeless relationship with the horse, "Cavalia" follows a subtle story line touching on the evolution of the horse from the wilderness to domestication and ultimately a new rapport with humans based on respect and freedom.

"I've never used traditional stages. I'm like an inventor of stages," explains Latourelle, who created a 150-foot wide rectangular stage for "Cavalia" that requires 800 tons of sand to prepare. Panoramic projections create an ever-changing backdrop for the cast of more than thirty-three horses and twenty-eight human performers.

Horses Rule

"I've always tried to reinvent the arts," notes Latourelle who long searched for opportunities to integrate horses into his shows before "Cavalia." The reality of a horse production has yielded its share of revelations. "I realized that making a creation with horses, the horse dictates the tempo. It slows down everything," notes Latourelle, who engaged the talents of Frédéric Pignon and Magali Delgado of France as "Cavalia's" Equestrian Co-Directors early on in the show's development, to participate in every step of the creation process. "When you work with just the human, you can go ten hours in a row with the same acrobat or dancer and still work. With horses, you have to pretty much follow their rules," adds Latourelle, who is clearly making plans for a long run.

"My dream, if my dream comes true, in fifty years you're going to open the dictionary and read the definition of 'Cavalia,' which would be the definition of our show," laughs

Latourelle. "I'm forty-eight now. So in fifty years, it will be for my two sons."

Horse Family

"When I see my horses it's like my children," describes the dark-haired Equestrian Co-Director Pignon, whose talent for training horses at liberty (free) is considered among the world's best. "We spend so much time together, every day. All the work that we do is around them. I could not do another job. It's impossible."

The thoughts of his wife and co-director mirror Pignon's own. "We had the same passion, we wanted to do shows together so we thought it would be a good idea to put our energies together and do something," says Delgado, an accomplished trainer and performer in her own right, whose parents breed Lusitano horses in the South of France. The attractive brunette continues, "We love our horses a lot. In France, we live with our horses. Our house is between the two stables. That's why we know every horse and training them is easy for us. We can train horses very fast, but we like to take our time." Half the equine cast in "Cavalia" was brought from France.

Through imperceptible body gestures, Pignon directs a lineup of loose stallions to lay down one by one in the show, to surround him in a tight-knit group, to rear together, and even to follow him with manners seemingly suitable for a black-tie event. His insights on horses are anything but expected from a person that many consider an authority on the subject.

"I think we don't know enough about horses. I think we're just discovering them," says Pignon. "Most of the people think they know enough to understand horses, but I think it's not true. We are just at the beginning of this research." Templado, a veteran Lusitano stallion performing in "Cavalia," whom Pignon has worked with for more than twelve years, significantly changed many previous perceptions for both him and his wife. "We had a philosophy about training, but when we met Templado he was like a teenager rebelling against everything. Sometimes he was aggressive, sometimes he was afraid. We had to learn to understand what he was trying to explain. He taught us a lot," remarks Pignon. "I think we have to learn more to be more attentive to the horses. They want to speak, they want to give more information, but we don't know how to read everything. We just know a little bit," he notes.

Pignon explains further, "When horses know we understand them, they give more and more information, but if they think we don't understand them, they won't. I've met a lot of horses that don't want to speak more with humans because they say, 'All humans are stupid, they don't understand nothing, and I don't speak more,'" continues Pignon, whom some term a "horse whisperer." He emphasizes, "We can say we love the horses, but if this is not true every day the horse knows. Horses are very honest with us so we have to be the same with them."

The Frenchman recalls meeting the legendary Hollywood horse trainer Corky Randall, several years before in Florida. "Every time he speaks about horses, it was just like a young man. I think when we've met people like this, we know we are the same family. The first time I met Corky, I didn't understand everything he said, my English was so bad. But when we worked with horses, we understood each other perfectly. He just had to look at me or give a little sign. Everybody thought it was very strange to see that. We could understand everything without words."

⌒ Try This

How well do you live your art? Do you dedicate your life to a passion? Would you dedicate your life to horses? Are you the same person "on stage" or "off," whatever that means in your life? Do you listen to an internal voice of timing or are you directed by an outer schedule of expectations and demands? Witnessing an equestrian theatrical performance may represent a life-altering experience. If such a thought captures your imagination, set out on a mission to accomplish your dream. The masters of this genre have created an equine art form.

Begin with a virtual trip to Théâter Zingaro at the troupe's home in Aubervilliers, France (a Paris suburb) at *www.theatre-zingaro.com*. Sites on the property (like the stable) are depicted, along with scenes from the current and previous productions. A tour schedule for "Loungta" is posted. Generally Zingaro performs at its home theater from November through February. (Note: Zingaro is not for young children or anyone who dislikes incense.) Have no fear, there are other options. See the Académie du Spectacle Equestre at the Grande Ecurie du Château de Versailles at *www.acadequestre.fr*. Details on applying for the Academy are on the Web site, along with information on viewing the morning training sessions in person. Versailles is easily accessible by train from Paris. For travel details on France, stop by *www.franceguide.com*. Meanwhile, keep an eye out for "Cavalia" as it tours North America. Visit *www.cavalia.net* to see when it's headed to a town near you. The production is geared to audiences of all ages. Considering it aims to make the dictionary, it will be touring for some time to come.